Hot Science is a s
and technology
dark matter to gene editing, these are books for popular
science readers who like to go that little bit deeper ...

AVAILABLE NOW AND COMING SOON:

Hot Science series editor: Brian Clegg

BEHAVIOURAL
ECONOMICS

BEHAVIOURAL ECONOMICS

**Psychology, neuroscience, and the
human side of economics**

DAVID ORRELL

ICON

Published in the UK and USA in 2021
by Icon Books Ltd, Omnibus Business Centre,
39–41 North Road, London N7 9DP
email: info@iconbooks.com
www.iconbooks.com

Sold in the UK, Europe and Asia
by Faber & Faber Ltd, Bloomsbury House,
74–77 Great Russell Street,
London WC1B 3DA or their agents

Distributed in the UK, Europe and Asia
by Grantham Book Services,
Trent Road, Grantham NG31 7XQ

Distributed in the USA
by Publishers Group West,
1700 Fourth Street, Berkeley, CA 94710

Distributed in Australia and New Zealand
by Allen & Unwin Pty Ltd,
PO Box 8500, 83 Alexander Street,
Crows Nest, NSW 2065

Distributed in South Africa
by Jonathan Ball, Office B4, The District,
41 Sir Lowry Road, Woodstock 7925

Distributed in India by Penguin Books India,
7th Floor, Infinity Tower – C, DLF Cyber City,
Gurgaon 122002, Haryana

Distributed in Canada by Publishers Group Canada,
76 Stafford Street, Unit 300
Toronto, Ontario M6J 2S1

ISBN: 978-178578-644-0

Typeset in Iowan by Marie Doherty

Printed and bound in Great Britain
by Clays Ltd, Elcograf S.p.A.

ABOUT THE AUTHOR

David Orrell is a scientist and writer of books on science and economics. His latest books are *Economyths: 11 Ways Economics Gets It Wrong* (Icon Books, 2017), and *Quantum Economics: The New Science of Money* (Icon Books, 2018).

CONTENTS

INTRODUCTION

This volume forms part of the 'Hot Science' series of books, and if there is one area of economics which would seem to qualify for that descriptor it is behavioural economics. Both because it is 'hot' – according to the American Economic Association, since 1995 the number of academic meetings on the topic has expanded by about a factor of ten – and because it is based on empirical science. The marriage of psychology, neuroscience, and economics, behavioural economics is an attempt to put the study of economic decision-making onto a firm scientific basis.

Economists had long assumed, if only to simplify their models, that people make decisions rationally in order to optimise their utility (i.e. happiness or pleasure). Here 'rational' doesn't mean sensible or reasonable, it just means acting in a way that is internally consistent. Psychologists, after many decades of the close study of actual human behaviour, had come to a rather different conclusion.

For example, far from being perfectly clear-sighted and rational, we are subject to numerous cognitive biases. In fact, identifying such biases has become something of a growth industry – Wikipedia currently lists about 200 of them, ranging from general ones like the default effect (given a number of options we tend to select the default one) to more specific ones such as the IKEA effect, which refers to 'The tendency for people to place a disproportionately high value on objects that they partially assembled themselves, such as furniture from IKEA, regardless of the quality of the end result' (a similar effect explains why cake mixes ask you to add an egg). Often these are combined, as when IKEA becomes the default option for home furnishing.

While some of these biases arise from the way we perceive the world and structure our thoughts as individuals, many are caused by social factors. Mainstream economics has traditionally treated people as the social equivalent of individual atoms, but behavioural economists argue that everything from the way we shop at the neighbourhood mall to the workings of the global financial system is shaped by the way we interact as groups. An example is the behaviour seen in stock markets, where investors frequently stampede in and out of the market in near-perfect synchrony like a startled herd of cattle.

One reason for these biases is that, far from being the computer-like *Homo economicus* of traditional economics, where every decision is based on Spock-like logic, we make most decisions based on heuristics – rules-of-thumb, like going for that default option, that provide a shortcut and allow us to protect our brains from too much demanding thought. It seems we are as stingy with our mental resources as we are with the physical kind. And when faced with complex questions with payoffs that are hard to compare, we often reinterpret the question by framing it in a particular way to make the decision easier – or allowing someone else, like a marketer or politician, to frame it for us.

Behavioural economics also raises other questions about the core ideas of economics, such as the thorny topic of utility. In traditional economics, people were assumed to have fixed preferences. The purpose of economic exchange was to optimise utility, which was a measure of how these preferences were met. Psychologists have long known, however, that our preferences are not set in stone, but change with time and with context. Utility is therefore not a stable or well-defined quantity, which as we will see has implications for how we model economic transactions. Behavioural effects also come into play in other areas such as finance or macroeconomics (the study of the economy as a whole), which have come under increasing scrutiny since the financial crisis of 2007–8.

Although its roots go back much further, behavioural economics as we know it today began with the work of small teams of psychologists in the 1970s. They were interested not in building a grand general theory of economics but in studying how people actually make decisions, through experiments where they enlisted subjects to play games or make choices. In the last few decades the field has become increasingly popular – publicised in books such as *Freakonomics* (2005) by economist Steven Levitt and journalist Stephen J. Dubner, *Nudge* (2008) by economist Richard H. Thaler and law professor Cass R. Sunstein, and *Thinking, Fast and Slow* (2011) by psychologist Daniel Kahneman – and has become a regular offering in university curricula. Its founders (including Thaler and Kahneman) have been garlanded with the Nobel Memorial Prize in Economic Sciences, which is the economics version of the Nobel Prize. However, as we'll see, the field also has its critics – such as forecasting expert Nassim Taleb who say it goes too far in attempting to model human psychology (he has described it as 'bullshit science'), and others who say it doesn't go far enough.

This book will take you on a guided tour of some of the murkier aspects of economic behaviour, and show how behavioural economics is putting the study of human nature back into economics, including shaping our response to some of our most pressing issues such as climate change and pandemics. The rest of the book can be divided roughly into three parts. Chapters 1 and 2 show how behavioural economics is affecting us today, and goes back to revisit how it first emerged as a contender to mainstream approaches. Chapters 3 to 6 focus on how people make decisions as individuals. We explore the various cognitive effects that sometimes confuse us, and the heuristics that get us through the day. Finally, Chapters 7 and 8 broaden the view to consider social behaviours such as herding and altruism, and show how these effects scale up to affect areas such as the stock market and the macroeconomy.

Along the way, we will look at some of the ways behavioural economics is used and abused by companies and governments, assess the strengths and weaknesses of the field, consider its effectiveness as a policy tool, and ask whether it represents a revolution in economics, or is best seen as an adjustment to existing practice. We begin in the next chapter by considering an archetypal illustration of the power, the challenges, and the limitations of behavioural economics.

STAY OR GO?

1

Many of the results in behavioural psychology are based, as we'll see, on the results of psychological experiments, in which human subjects are asked to reveal their preferences by answering a kind of survey. In June 2016 the UK population was asked, in a large and binding version of such a survey, to answer the following economics-related question: 'Should the United Kingdom remain a member of the European Union or leave the European Union?'

The choice was stark – as The Clash once sang, 'should I stay or should I go?' – but the potential payoffs were complex and hard to compare. And the event, including its build-up and aftermath, either involved or illustrated behavioural economics at almost every level. (British readers may be tired of the topic, but be assured that the focus here is on the behavioural aspects, not rehashing the politics!)

The referendum was famously announced by then-Prime Minister David Cameron in early 2016. Cameron was no stranger to behavioural economics. Members of his Conservative Party leadership team had met with economist

Richard Thaler in 2008, and decided, according to Thaler, that his behavioural approach to public policy 'was one that the party could support as part of a rebranding ... to make the party more progressive and pro-environment'. And perhaps it could help to smooth the effects of the austerity measures which had been imposed by his government following the financial crisis.

In 2010 Cameron set up the Behavioural Insights Team, otherwise known as the Nudge Unit, in an effort to incorporate its insights into government policy. One of the Nudge Unit's first wins was to reword tax collection letters to include a phrase saying that 'the great majority of people in the UK pay their taxes on time', which shamed people into paying and increased the compliance rate by about 5 per cent. Sending reminders by text message helped too. (Though as Levitt and Stephen Dubner note in their book *Think Like a Freak*, Cameron's interest in their ideas didn't extend to healthcare – when they suggested in a meeting that the NHS shouldn't be free, he walked out.)

Cameron at the time had a problem with Eurosceptics in his party, who maintained a Thatcherite distrust of what former leader Margaret Thatcher had called a 'European super-state' and favoured traditional free-market economics with minimal state intervention. On the other hand, he was also in political trouble with the electorate because of the unpopular austerity measures, which involved shrinking government services.

Rather than confront the Eurosceptics directly, Cameron promised during the run-up to the 2015 general election that, if the Conservatives were elected with a majority, then he would hold a referendum on EU membership. This was what behavioural scientists call a *risky decision under uncertainty* but it seemed like a relatively safe gamble, since the Conservatives were then in a coalition government and few political forecasters expected them to win a majority. It was also an illustration of what behavioural economists call *present bias*, where Cameron chose a short-term solution for boosting his support in the party over the long-term risk that the whole thing might blow up in his face.

When to the surprise of most forecasters and commentators the Conservatives won a majority, Cameron had to hold the referendum, but campaigned for the Remain side, which was a little confusing since he had previously presented himself as being somewhat of a sceptic (behavioural economists call this *preference reversal*, which is particularly popular with politicians). Like most of the Europhiles, he also seemed optimistic that Remain would comfortably prevail (as we will see, *optimism bias* affects not just our political leaders). This was backed by political forecasters and commentators who confidently predicted a Remain victory (we also experience an *overconfidence effect* when it comes to our ability to predict the future). And of course, the population was always susceptible to a bit of *nudging*.

Project Fear

In order to help cement the anticipated result, the Chancellor George Osborne penned his own forecast of the possible outcomes, presenting the choice in starkly simple economic terms. In a Treasury analysis on the economic impact of leaving the EU, he wrote that were the country to vote Leave, the 'central estimate was that Britain would be permanently poorer by the equivalent of £4,300 per household by 2030 and every year thereafter'. In the short term, 'a vote to leave would represent an immediate and profound shock to our economy. That shock would push our economy into a recession and lead to an increase in unemployment of around 500,000, GDP would be 3.6% smaller, average real wages would be lower, inflation higher, sterling weaker, house prices would be hit and public borrowing would rise compared with a vote to remain.' (*Framing* the issue in this way appealed directly to the electorate's *loss aversion*, which is our tendency to overweight potential losses as compared to gains when making decisions.)

In contrast, Osborne wrote, a vote to remain 'would be the best way to ensure continued growth and safeguard jobs, providing security for working people now and opportunity for the next generation. This document,' he wrote, 'provides the facts that I hope the people of Britain will consider when they make this historic decision one month from today.' Or as Cameron summarised, 'Stay in and you know what you'll get.'

This in turn was an appeal to *status quo bias* which is our tendency to stay with the devil we know rather than the one we don't. As the behavioural economist Michael Sherman explained, 'There's a very large irrational bias people have called status quo bias ... And Prime Minister Cameron knows that.' In an interview, Thaler said, 'I am not a prognosticator, but I would bet on them staying. And I think that there is a tendency, when push comes to shove, to stick with the status quo.'

The argument was therefore a combination of traditional economic reasoning, with a good dose of fear – its alarmist claims of economic calamity soon earned the Remain campaign the name 'Project Fear' – and a reminder of the relative safety and security of keeping things as they are. Decision-making has two components, the objective and the subjective, and Cameron and his team were targeting both.

However, in many ways Cameron and Osborne – representing a certain type of Conservative whose political viewpoint was pretty much based on the concepts of loss aversion and status quo bias – were out-of-touch with the electorate. Not everyone worried about a weaker sterling, or London house prices, or public borrowing, or abstract measures of economic growth like gross domestic product (GDP), especially when they had little apparent local relevance. As one heckler told a Europe expert, 'That's your bloody GDP. Not ours.' Loss aversion and status quo bias are less effective when you don't feel like you are winning under the status quo. And while Cameron et al were busy framing the referendum in terms of money and economics, the Leave campaign was framing it in terms of something even more basic, which is identity.

The experts

The Leave campaign did make some loss-framed economic arguments, for example in claiming that £350 million was being sent to the EU every week. This number sounded bigger than Osborne's £4,300 per household per year, even though it was actually six times smaller (the way that numbers are presented affects how we judge them). However, a number of polls conducted just after the referendum showed that, while Remainers listed the main reason for their vote as 'the economy', those who voted Leave listed 'sovereignty' and 'immigration' as their main concerns. For these Leavers, the referendum tapped into fundamental questions about what Britain represented, which politicians and others were happy to exploit. The government was about to be out-nudged.

In a May 2016 article for the *Telegraph*, future Prime Minister Boris Johnson argued that the end goal of the European Union was to create a European superstate 'just as Hitler did', while in contrast Churchill's 'vision for Britain was not subsumed within a European superstate'. The Leave argument was summed up in the slogan 'Take Back Control' which similarly seemed to hark back to the days of the British Empire. Dominic Cummings, who oversaw the campaign, later said that he began with 'Take Control' but changed it to 'Take Back Control' because it 'plays into a strong evolved instinct – we hate losing things, especially control'.

Experts on the Remain side could throw scary statistics around with abandon, but as Michael Gove, who campaigned for Leave, put it, 'I think people in this country have had enough of experts.' And while few voters would claim to be able to follow the economic calculations of either side, it was much easier to say whether you were for or against immigration. Faced with a complicated comparison where there is no easy answer, we often resort to shorthand responses, such as substituting the original question with another one (behavioural psychologists call this the *attribute substitution heuristic*).

However, while the people may have had enough of experts, another kind of expert – the behavioural sort – had plenty of time for *them*. As we will see in this book, while behavioural economics is often associated with government interventions, in many ways it is like a particularly scientific-looking version of marketing theory – and unless perhaps you live in China, where the Communist Party controls much of the news and social media, and is developing a social credit system to reward good behaviour and punish bad, private companies are often much more adept at nudging people than the state is.

Triggered

The now-defunct firm Cambridge Analytica, for example, took behavioural approaches to a whole new level. The company was part-owned by Robert Mercer, the billionaire CEO of hedge fund Renaissance Technologies, who had turned his talents from predicting markets to shaping them through organisations and causes including Breitbart News, Donald Trump's presidential campaign, and Brexit. Cambridge Analytica used an online psychological profile app to get profiles of tens of millions of Facebook users, via a university researcher who had claimed to be using the data for academic purposes. The app was designed to assess people on the basis of five personality traits known as OCEAN: Openness, Conscientiousness, Extroversion, Agreeableness, and Neuroticism. Users were asked to read a series of statements like 'I am the life of the party' and rate them on a scale from very inaccurate to very accurate.

Psychologists use such quizzes in order to explore how personality shapes our decisions, including on how to vote. Importantly, though, the app also extracted data including likes and personal information from the test-taker's Facebook account. This vastly magnified the amount of data on which to train the artificial intelligence algorithms used to make predictions. The result was that Cambridge Analytica had a way to find 'persuadable' voters and identify emotional triggers. Someone who rated highly in neuroticism, say, might be easily manipulated through targeted ads featuring images of immigrants swarming into the country. According to Dominic Cummings, Vote Leave used this information to serve some 1.5 billion ads to 7 million people whom the algorithm had identified as 'persuadable' or 'shy' voters. The effort was concentrated at the end of the campaign as 'adverts are more effective the closer to the decision moment they hit the brain'. Behavioural psychologists refer to this as the *availability heuristic*.

The referendum was held on Friday 24 June 2016. When the results were tallied, a 51.9 per cent majority had voted Leave versus 48.1 per cent on the side of Remain. Cameron immediately resigned as Prime Minister, the pound saw its biggest ever daily fall against the US dollar, and Scottish First Minister Nicola Sturgeon announced Scotland's desire to remain a part of the EU (reflecting how the majority had voted north of the border). Meanwhile a Google Trends report from the day of the vote showed that 'What is the EU?' was the second most searched-for phrase about the European Union.

The forecasters and commentators who had continued to believe in a Remain victory until the last moment were in shock. This despite the fact that a number of polls suggested that the Leave campaign was ahead. (As we'll see, behavioural effects continue to befuddle forecasters.)

A breakdown of the results showed that young, mobile, educated people – especially those clustered in the financial and business hub of London – were the most likely to vote Remain, which was unsurprising given that they had the most to benefit from EU integration. However, other

STAY OR GO? 13

results were more confusing from the perspective of traditional economics. Rational choice theory would suggest
that areas such as Wales would have been pro-EU because
they had received visible benefits in the form of subsidies
and projects, and there were relatively few immigrants, yet
the locals came out strongly for Leave. But what counts is
not just absolute levels, but a sense of relative change –
and even low levels of immigration can be enough to evoke
resistance.

Hypernudge

While the Brexit referendum will probably be discussed
and argued over for years, what is clear is that the vote
both exposed and created deep divisions within the British
population, and the ongoing debates caused what many commentators described as something akin to a collective mental
breakdown. It also raised questions about things as basic as
personal autonomy and the democratic process. With both
private companies, and state actors such as Russia and China
trying to manipulate us online, it has become customary
today to wonder whether elections have been hacked, not
so much by hacking the computers which tally the results,
but by using behavioural techniques and insights to hack
the brains of voters. The accuracy of the algorithms used by
Vote Leave can be debated (and no amount of advertising on
Facebook or elsewhere could help Michael Bloomberg in his
failed bid to become the 2020 Democratic candidate in the
US), but the reason Facebook is one of the most profitable
companies on the planet is because of the value contained in
its data, which suggests this data has some use to marketers.

As we will see in the next chapter, the study of economic behaviour has its roots in military research, and today it has been weaponised into a tool of political and corporate manipulation.

The results of the referendum also provided a graphic illustration of how behavioural effects make the economy so difficult to predict. In the months after the referendum, the UK economy performed far better than most forecasters, including those at the Bank of England, had expected. The supposedly 'irrational' voters may have been right to reject expert claims of impending disaster, especially given the poor track record of economic forecasting. It was only years later, as the uncertainty wore on, that the economy seemed to be affected. One of the biggest lessons of behavioural economics may be that we need to be more humble about our understanding of the economy.

The success of behavioural economics and techniques such as social nudging has also led to a backlash. In 2019 the computer analyst whistleblower Edward Snowden warned that 'new platforms and algorithms' have given governments and corporations the power to 'monitor and record private activities of people' in such a way that 'they're able to shift our behavior. In some cases they're able to predict our decisions – and also nudge them – to different outcomes. And they do this by exploiting the human need for belonging.' He described the result as 'the most effective means of social control in the history of our species'. Karen Yeung of Birmingham Law School coined the term 'hypernudge' to describe nudges based on big data analytics that 'are extremely powerful and potent due to their networked, continuously updated, dynamic and pervasive nature'.

At the same time, the picture of all-knowing technocrats gently nudging, sheepdog-style, the populace into the right decisions has also taken a bit of a hit. When the legal scholar and behavioural economist Carl Sunstein served as officer of the Office of Information and Regulatory Affairs under US President Barack Obama, he encouraged 'clear, simple, salient, and meaningful disclosures', and recommended that 'presentation greatly matters; if, for example, a potential outcome is framed as a loss, it may have more impact than if it is presented as a gain.' Donald Trump took the second point at least to heart, though not perhaps in the way that Sunstein would have expected. And groups like the anti-vaccination movement thrive on complicated theories and the sowing of doubt, not clear information.

Behavioural economics exists at the nexus between psychology, politics, and money. And while the Brexit referendum was a something of a one-off event (probably), we are faced with the same kind of choice between 'hard' abstract prices and 'soft' but tangible emotions every time we make an economic transaction, whether it is buying a house, or selling an heirloom at a yard sale. In the next chapter, we take a step back, and ask how economics got along before the psychologists came on board – and why the behavioural approach was perceived as such a shock.

Mindspace

The MINDSPACE framework was developed in 2010 by the Cabinet Office and the Institute for Government as a way to raise awareness among UK civil servants of 'nine of the most robust (non-coercive) influences on our behaviour'.

We reproduce it here so that, if you ever think you're being manipulated by the government, you can just check against this list. Source: Cabinet Office/Institute for Government (2010).

Messenger	We are heavily influenced by who communicates information
Incentives	Our responses to incentives are shaped by predictable mental shortcuts such as strongly avoiding losses
Norms	We are strongly influenced by what others do
Defaults	We 'go with the flow' of pre-set options
Salience	Our attention is drawn to what is novel and seems relevant to us
Priming	Our acts are often influenced by sub-conscious cues
Affect	Our emotional associations can powerfully shape our actions
Commitments	We seek to be consistent with our public promises, and reciprocate acts
Ego	We act in ways that make us feel better about ourselves.

THE RATIONAL(ISH) ANIMAL

2

Behavioural economics is often portrayed as being a little radical and carrying a whiff of danger. The subtitle of *Freakonomics* was 'A Rogue Economist Explores the Hidden Side of Everything'. In his 2015 book *Misbehaving*, Richard Thaler wrote of the field's 'heresy' in questioning mainstream authority, and the danger of dabbling in 'treacherous, inflammatory territory'. Behavioural economists like to see themselves as the teen rebels of economics.

To a non-economist, though, it might seem strange that bringing psychology into economics could be viewed as a heretical pursuit or a sign of roguish tendencies. After all, isn't economics a social science like any other, that is ultimately about human behaviour, and that should therefore be open to incorporating experimental evidence from related fields? As the investor Charlie Munger put it in a 1995 speech: 'How could economics not be behavioral? If it isn't behavioral, what the hell is it?'

To understand why behavioural economics has been considered so radical, it is first necessary to understand how economics was before it came along. This chapter will therefore give a brief overview of the traditional mainstream approach which has dominated economics for about the last 150 years, highlight some of the key differences with the behavioural perspective, and show how behavioural economics emerged as an alternative.

The calculus of economics

If there is one thing that captures the essence of the mainstream approach towards human behaviour, it is an emphasis on self-interested rationality. The idea goes back to Aristotle who saw the rational principle as the secret sauce which distinguished mankind from animals. It was satirised by Bertrand Russell in 1950 when he wrote: 'Man is a rational animal – so at least I have been told. Throughout a long life, I have looked diligently for evidence in favour of this statement, but so far I have not had the good fortune to come across it, though I have searched in many countries spread over three continents.' Not being prone to that kind of empirical research, the early economists did find it, in an imaginary creature called *Homo economicus*, or rational economic man.

The founder of economics as we know it today is usually considered to be Adam Smith. Smith was inspired by the physical theories of Isaac Newton and in his 1776 book *The Wealth of Nations* tried to put economics onto a similarly scientific plane. The best-known aspect of his book is what became known as the 'invisible hand' which acted as a kind of feedback that regulated market prices. If prices were too high, then new suppliers would enter the market, driving the price down; conversely, if prices were too low, suppliers would leave or go broke. Prices would always therefore be restored to the 'natural price' which would reflect the cost of production, as an automatic result of people's self-interest: 'It is not from the benevolence of the butcher, the brewer, or the baker that we expect our dinner, but from their regard to their own interest. We address ourselves, not to their humanity but to their self-love.'

While early classical economists such as Smith didn't assume that people were entirely rational – only that they were driven by self-interest – this changed in the nineteenth century with the arrival of neoclassical economists (as they became known) whose aim was to mathematicise the field, and whose work shaped mainstream economics as it is today. A first step was to be more precise about what exactly people were doing when they engaged in economic transactions – in other words, what was driving them. Smith had associated intrinsic value with the cost of production. Gold, for example, was worth a lot because it was hard to dig up (even though in practice most of the work at the time was done by slaves). For neoclassical economists such as William Stanley Jevons, the answer was instead found in the philosopher Jeremy Bentham's idea of utility, defined as that which appears to 'augment or diminish the happiness of the party whose interest is in question'.

According to Bentham, the pleasure or pain of an event depended on a number of factors, including its intensity, its duration, and its certainty or uncertainty. From the point of view of economics, as Jevons pointed out, this meant that utility had two dimensions, corresponding to power and duration – just as our electricity bill depends on the power consumed by light bulbs, and the amount of time we leave them on. It also meant that utility had a probabilistic aspect to it. 'When it is as likely as not that I shall receive £100,' wrote Jevons, 'the chance is worth but £50, because if, for a great many times in succession, I purchase the chance at this rate, I shall almost certainly neither lose nor gain.'

The task for economists was therefore well-defined: 'Pleasure and pain are undoubtedly the ultimate objects of the Calculus of Economics. To satisfy our wants to the utmost with the least effort – to procure the greatest amount of what is desirable at the expense of the least that is undesirable – in other words, to maximise pleasure, is the problem of Economics.' Society's purpose, meanwhile, was to satisfy Bentham's 'greatest happiness principle' – i.e. provide the greatest happiness to the most people. The goodness of an action was simply the sum of its positive and negative effects on the people involved. Jevons used this definition of utility to derive relationships such as his 'equation of exchange', which states that for a consumer to be maximising his or her utility, the ratio of the marginal utility (i.e. the utility of purchasing one extra unit) of each item consumed to its price must be equal. For example, if you want an orange twice as much as you want an apple, but the orange also costs twice as much, then buying one or the other will have the same effect on net utility.

Measuring happiness

Of course, this theory raised the question of how utility was to be measured. After all, it isn't easy to put a number on pleasure. In an 1884 paper titled 'What is an emotion?' the psychologist Richard James suggested that emotional states could be linked – via the autonomic nervous system – to measurable physical symptoms such as sweating or pulse rate. The physician Ernst Weber, who along with his student Gustav Fechner was a founder of experimental psychology, performed a series of experiments to tease out empirical rules for things like our sensitivity to different sensations. One result was his theory of the just-noticeable difference, which says that a change in stimuli – for example, the weight of a barbell we are holding – has to be about 8 to 10 per cent in order for us to notice it. In other words, what counts is not the magnitude of the effect, but the proportional change relative to a reference point. This behavioural rule, known as Weber's law (or sometimes the Weber–Fechner law since Fechner derived the mathematical expression), is often applied in marketing and affects things like how we perceive a change in prices – a change of less than 10 per cent is usually small enough to avoid exciting customers into complaining.

Inspired by the findings of 'psychophysics' as it became known, the nineteenth-century economist Francis Edgeworth suggested the use of a hedonimeter which would register 'the height of pleasure experienced by an individual' or more technically 'the psychical side of a physical change in what may be dimly discerned as a sort of hedonico-magnetic field' (patent still pending, most likely). Today, cognitive neuroscientists have a variety of tools to measure our responses, including brain scans showing which parts of our brains are being activated (and Amazon is reported to be working on a wrist-worn, voice-activated device that can read human emotions).

Economists such as Edgeworth assumed that what counted was the total pain experienced over time (in mathematical terms, the integral). However, one finding from tests done on people undergoing painful medical procedures is that there is a distinction between experienced pain and remembered pain. When asked how painful a procedure has been, patients tend to focus on a combination of the maximum pain experienced and the pain experienced at the end (i.e. the most recent), rather than the duration of the pain. If the goal is to reduce the negative memory, then long but less painful appears to beat short but more painful. In the same way, experiments on rats involving electrical stimulation of their brains' pleasure centres showed that the appeal depended only on the peak intensity, not the duration.

Back in the nineteenth century, while neoclassical economists associated utility with a kind of psychic energy, measuring it certainly wasn't straightforward. No one even knew what units it should have (though 'utils' is sometimes used). Fortunately, economists had an answer to these problems, which is that there was already an exquisitely sensitive device that could measure happiness. It was called the market.

The market pendulum

The shift from a labour theory of value to one based on utility was motivated in part by the growing size and influence of financial markets. If you own a stock, and it doubles in price, then your utility has gone up – no labour required. And if Smith was right that the invisible hand of the markets drove prices to a level which correctly reflected their intrinsic value, and neoclassical economists were right that intrinsic value reflected utility, then it followed that utility could be inferred directly from market price.

Or as William Stanley Jevons put it: 'I hesitate to say that men will ever have the means of measuring directly the feelings of the human heart … but, just as we measure gravity by its effects in the motion of a pendulum, so we may estimate the equality or inequality of feelings by the decisions of the human mind. The will is our pendulum, and its oscillations are minutely registered in the price lists of the markets.' The units of utility were therefore units of currency.

Of course, this theory would only work if the decisions people were making were actually the right ones. Jevons therefore assumed, as the economics professor Bert Mosselmans summarises, that 'economic agents are perfectly rational, perfectly foresighted and in possession of perfect information'. Neoclassical economics therefore did have a theory of human behaviour, it was just a rather strange (and flattering) one. (Jevons also wrote a book about logic, and invented a kind of early computer called the logic piano, which would have been helpful for those struggling to attain perfect rationality and foresight.)

In an 1898 essay titled 'Why is Economics not an Evolutionary Science?', the economist Thorstein Veblen memorably mocked this particular behavioural model: 'The hedonistic conception of man is that of a lightning calculator of pleasures and pains, who oscillates like a homogeneous globule of desire of happiness under the impulse of stimuli that shift him about the area but leave him intact.' Nietzsche had a shot at the utilitarians as well in his 1886 book *Beyond Good and Evil*: 'Not one of all these ponderous herd animals with their uneasy conscience (who undertake to advocate the cause of egoism as the cause of the general welfare –) wants to know or scent that the "general welfare" is not an ideal, or a goal, or a concept that can be grasped at all, but only an emetic …'

But while this view of humanity may have been rather unrealistic, it certainly made it much easier to build sophisticated models of the economy, because all that mattered was prices. The French economist Leon Walras, for example, built a model of a market economy which showed how prices were driven to an equilibrium level. This model formed the basis for the modern equilibrium models discussed later.

The emphasis on numerical prices, as opposed to psychological realism, also lent the field of economics an imposing air of mathematical rigour. As the British economist Lionel Robbins wrote in 1932, its findings were based on 'deduction from simple assumptions reflecting very elementary facts of general experience' and as such were 'as universal as the laws of mathematics or mechanics, and as little capable of "suspension"'. Economists soon lost interest in talking about the qualities of human emotions, and switched to working with preferences, which simply rank things or desires in order. Over time, as behavioural economist John Tomer notes, neoclassical economists 'were able to rid economics of practically all its explicit ties to psychology'.

Economists also distanced themselves from the ideal of rational economic man, claiming that their models were actually much more sophisticated. As Robbins argued, 'if it were generally realised that Economic Man is only an expository device – a first approximation used very cautiously at one stage in the development of arguments which, in their full development, neither employ any such assumption nor demand it in any way for a justification of their procedure – it is improbable that he would be such a universal bogey.'

In reality, though, economics was about to take the concept of rationality to a whole new level – and rational economic man was going to get super powers, thanks to a mathematician with super powers of his own.

Axiomatise this

John von Neumann is considered to be one of the most important and influential mathematicians of all time. During his career, which combined pure and applied research, he made major contributions to areas including pure mathematics, quantum physics, computing, weather forecasting, and economics. If there was anyone who could put economics onto a firm mathematical basis, it was him.

As a seventeen-year-old mathematical prodigy growing up in Hungary, von Neumann had attempted to tackle one of the biggest problems in mathematics, which was how to prove that mathematics itself is a logical system based on a finite set of self-evident axioms. After seven years of work, it seemed he had succeeded in coming up with an unassailable proof – but just as mathematicians around the world were celebrating the apparent breakthrough, in 1931 the Austrian mathematician Kurt Gödel proved that mathematics was incomplete. For any set of axioms, there will always be a statement that cannot be proved to be true or false without adding another axiom.

Von Neumann then turned his attention to quantum theory. At the time, there were two mathematical approaches to the subject, developed by the German physicist Werner Heisenberg and the Austrian physicist Erwin Schrödinger. The two frameworks seemed to be inconsistent, but von Neumann showed they were one and the same. This was a great achievement – but this time von Neumann's thunder was stolen by the English physicist Paul Dirac, whose proof was more accessible to physicists.

Next up for the von Neumann treatment was economics. After learning through a friend, the economist and fellow

Hungarian Nicholas Kaldor, about Walras' *Elements of Pure Economics*, von Neumann realised that economic transactions were a kind of game, where the buyer and seller each adopted strategies to optimise their utility – and perhaps a theory of such games too could be reduced to a single set of consistent axioms. Working with the economist Oskar Morgenstern, he began work on a paper which eventually became the 600-page *Theory of Games and Economic Behaviour*. The aim was 'to find the mathematically complete principles which define "rational behavior" for the participants in a social economy, and to derive from them the general characteristics of that behavior'. Key to their argument was the theory of expected utility, which laid out four axioms which defined a rational decision-maker.

Suppose an agent is faced with two lotteries, A and B, with different potential payoffs. Here a lottery refers not just to the kind you buy a ticket for in the hope of becoming a millionaire, but any choice where the outcome is uncertain, such as Brexit. The Completeness axiom assumes that the agent has well-defined preferences and can always choose between the two alternatives. The Transitivity axiom assumes that the agent always makes decisions consistently – if they prefer A now, they will prefer it tomorrow. The Independence axiom assumes that, if the agent prefers A over B, then introducing an unrelated lottery C does not change that preference. Finally, the Continuity axiom assumes that if the agent prefers A over B, and B over C, then there should be some mix of the most-favoured A and the least-favoured C which is equally as attractive as B. If the agent meets these four axioms, then their preferences can be modelled using a so-called utility function, and they are officially rational.

As Jevons had pointed out, the utility we expected to

derive from a transaction also had a probabilistic element. In game theory, as von Neumann and Morgenstern called their creation, the 'expected utility' is the utility of a lottery payout, multiplied by the probability of the payout. If the game is a coin toss, and the payout is a pound on heads and zero on tails, then the expected utility is 50p since there is a 50 per cent chance of winning the prize.

The book, when it came out in 1944, was an academic and popular hit – the *American Mathematical Society Bulletin* called it 'one of the major scientific contributions of the first half of the twentieth century' and the *New York Times* featured it on the front page of its 10 March 1946 Sunday edition, with the headline: 'A new approach to economic analysis that seeks to solve hitherto insoluble problems of business strategy by developing and applying to them a new mathematical theory of games of strategy like poker, chess and solitaire has caused a sensation among professional economists.'

Buoyed by this tremendous success, von Neumann and others immediately set about performing a series of exhaustive tests on experimental subjects in order to confirm their theory. No, they didn't! That task of performing empirical research on how people actually behave would be left to behavioural psychologists much later. Instead, working together with military strategists at the RAND Corporation, von Neumann tried out his theory on something much more exciting – nuclear war.

It's a MAD world

Using his game theory, von Neumann could determine the conditions under which the possible outcomes of a particular game would attain a stable and optimal solution. At the time, the US and Russia were engaged in a particularly high-stakes game known as the Cold War. The US had already used nuclear weapons, and Russia was developing them. What were the possible outcomes?

Having made important contributions to the development of the first nuclear weapons, von Neumann was a member of the US Atomic Energy Commission and advisor to President Eisenhower on the use of the bomb – so this wasn't a theoretical exercise. In fact, for him it was the ideal application for game theory.

In this case the 'game' can be viewed as an example of the prisoner's dilemma game, which was first invented at RAND in 1950, and is a staple of behavioural psychology. The prisoner's dilemma involves two imaginary criminals who have been arrested for a crime and held separately. One option for the prosecutor is to give each a reduced charge with a penalty of one year. However, if he can make one testify against the other, then he can obtain a three-year sentence for the accused party. He therefore offers each prisoner a choice: testify that the other person committed the crime, or remain silent. The rules are then as follows: if both prisoners remain silent, they both get one year on the lesser charge. If both prisoners betray the other, they both get two years. If only one prisoner betrays the other, he gets off and the other gets the full three years.

Applying game theory, we see that if a prisoner chooses to not testify, then the sentence is either one or three years (see Table 1). If we assume each is equally likely, then the expected sentence is two years. On the other hand, if he chooses to betray the other person, then his sentence is either zero years or two years, with an expected sentence of one year. In order to maximise his expected utility – i.e. reduce his expected sentence – the rational prisoner will therefore choose to betray.

Table 1. Possible moves for the prisoner's dilemma game. Each prisoner has the option to testify against the other prisoner, or remain silent.

Prisoner A strategy	Prisoner B strategy	Prisoner A sentence	Prisoner B sentence
silent	silent	1	1
silent	testify	3	0
testify	silent	0	3
testify	testify	2	2

In real life, the game becomes more complicated because agents might be thinking about what happens once they are released from prison. The political scientist James Der Derian taught the game to convicts from Gardner State Prison in a world politics class he was holding there, and found that they based their decision on established prison norms such as 'traditional codes of silence, pre-scripted stories, and intersubjective rituals of honor'. Even in lab experiments, 40–50 per cent of players choose to cooperate with the other prisoner and remain silent.

Applying this logic to the Cold War, though, each side had a choice to cooperate (not blow each other up) or defect (blow the other side up). The main difference is that in this case, there is perhaps less concern about what happens when you get out of prison, because the prison gets blown up too.

As von Neumann counselled the president, the logic was unassailable – the US should strike immediately, before Russia had the chance to develop its own weapon. That was the only winning strategy. However, while von Neumann managed to convince the secretary of state, John Foster Dulles, Eisenhower hesitated. And when the Russians announced in 1949 that they too had a bomb, it was too late.

Instead of nuclear Armageddon, the Cold War became a stand-off characterised by another strategy from game theory which became known as Mutually Assured Destruction, or MAD (von Neumann is said to have had a hand in the name, and he had a way with acronyms – he worked on an early computer called the Mathematical Analyser, Numerator, Integrator and Calculator, aka MANIAC). It is chilling to think that a belief in human logic could have come so close to destroying the world. Though as we'll see later, the same belief also came close to destroying the world financial system.

Rationalising the economy

Another aspect of the Cold War was the ideological and technological battle with the Soviet Union, and here again rational economic man had a role to play. As part of this effort, the US Department of Defense helped fund a range of scientific areas, including economics. The economists Kenneth Arrow and Gérard Debreu, who had worked with RAND and were funded in part by grants from the Office of Naval Research, combined a Walrasian model of a market economy with a result from game theory to 'prove' that a market economy would naturally drive prices to a stable equilibrium. The resulting equilibrium state furthermore satisfied a condition known as Pareto optimality – a weak kind of optimality which states that nothing can be changed without making at least one person worse off.

This result soon became known as the 'invisible hand theorem' and was popular with its military backers because it seemed to provide a mathematical proof that free-market capitalism was superior to communism. It also inspired the development of elaborate general equilibrium models of the economy, versions of which are still relied on by policymakers today. However, the proof relied on the powers of rational economic man being extended so that they included things like infinite computational power and the ability to devise plans for every future eventuality. Far from being just an 'expository device' as Robbins had claimed, rational economic man was gaining super powers and helping to win the Cold War.

In fact, rational economic man was just getting going. As we'll see later, Eugene Fama's efficient market made him the central plank of finance. Rational choice theory extended his influence into other areas such as psychology, sociology, and politics. As Gary Becker wrote in his 1976 book *The Economic Approach to Human Behavior*, 'the combined assumptions of maximizing behavior, market equilibrium, and stable preferences, used relentlessly and consistently form the heart of the economic approach … I have come to the position that the economic approach is a comprehensive one that is applicable to all human behavior.'

However, one of our 'irrational' biases is our tendency to rationalise, in order to make sense of the world and our own actions. No one gets fired for being too rational. And theories often seem less about understanding or predicting the world than about explaining it in terms of a particular worldview.

As Becker wrote those words, though, a new economic approach to human behaviour was already being formulated. In 1974, two psychologists, Daniel Kahneman and Amos

Tversky, published a paper in *Science* called 'Judgment Under Uncertainty: Heuristics and Biases'. They followed it up with other works including, in 1979, the paper 'Prospect Theory: An Analysis of Decision under Risk', which began:

> Expected utility theory has dominated the analysis of decision making under risk. It has been generally accepted as a normative model of rational choice, and widely applied as a descriptive model of economic behavior. Thus, it is assumed that all reasonable people would wish to obey the axioms of the theory, and that most people actually do, most of the time. The present paper describes several classes of choice problems in which preferences systematically violate the axioms of expected utility theory. In the light of these observations we argue that utility theory, as it is commonly interpreted and applied, is not an adequate descriptive model and we propose an alternative account of choice under risk.

And with those words, it can be said that behavioural economics as we know it today first broke into the economic consciousness.

TOO MUCH INFORMATION

3

Behavioural economics didn't spring fully formed from the void, and many of the ideas had already been around in one form or another. The problem was that they had failed to catch on with economists.

Starting in the 1950s, the economist and cognitive psychologist Herbert Simon had already begun to look at ways to bring psychology back into economics. According to Simon, while the 'classical theory of omniscient rationality is strikingly simple and beautiful' it had a little problem, which was that it didn't apply to the real world.* Expected utility theory assumed that people had stable preferences and could calculate both the utility and the odds of different outcomes. But in most real-life situations, it is impossible to make such calculations. Decision-makers therefore couldn't apply the theory. Instead they aimed to take reasonable decisions, by limiting their choices to a small set of alternatives, using

---

* For a discussion of the role of aesthetics in science, see my book *Truth or Beauty: Science and the Quest for Order*.

heuristics or rules-of-thumb, and by 'satisficing' – i.e. choosing an option that is 'good enough' as opposed to optimal.
Finally, they relied on judgement and intuition, as in the 'aha'
moment where the correct solution suddenly falls into place.

According to Simon, economists should therefore treat
people as 'boundedly rational' in the sense that they make
decisions subject to cognitive and behavioural limitations.
For example, rather than compute an employee's correct salary, an employer will just follow what is conventional, with
small adjustments. Instead of working out which product
on offer at a store is optimal, we choose one we have used
before. And we also learn from our mistakes and adjust our
behaviour over time.

While these ideas seem a perfectly reasonable description of human behaviour, as we have seen, they were out of
step with trends at the time. So, although Simons was later
awarded the Nobel Memorial Prize in economics, this aspect
of his work had little impact on the course of economics,
at least at the time. As Simons noted in his Nobel lecture,
'there was a vigorous reaction that sought to defend classical
theory from behavioralism on methodological grounds', in
large part because it didn't fit well with the increased math-
ematisation of economics. That problem was addressed by
Kahneman and Tversky, who found a way to integrate their
work in psychology with economics – in part, as we will see
later, by some clever branding.

The illusion of validity

Daniel Kahneman's interest in cognitive psychology dated
back to 1955, when, while working as a psychologist for the

Israeli army, he was tasked with finding out which soldiers would make good officers. The method he used, which was based on ones developed by the British Army in the Second World War, involved what looked like an ingenious experiment. Men were divided into groups of eight, with their insignia removed to conceal rank, and instructed to lift a telephone pole over a six-foot wall, without them or the pole touching the wall. Those who proved good at coordinating the others to get the job done obviously had the right stuff and were recommended for officer school.

Kahneman received monthly feedback on the progress of his recruits, and it soon became apparent that success at this 'Leaderless Group Challenge' was not a good predictor of success in the army. Or as Kahneman later put it, 'there was absolutely no relationship between what we saw and what people saw who examined them for six months in officer training school.'

But the interesting thing was that, even for a trained scientist like himself, this information made no difference to his own behaviour: 'The next day after getting those statistics, we put them there in front of the wall, gave them a telephone pole, and we were just as convinced as ever that we knew what kind of officer they were going to be.'

Kahneman continued to think about this after he moved to the United States in the late 1960s, where he began a long academic collaboration with the psychologist Amos Tversky. Their interest in economics was sparked by an essay from the Swiss economist Bruno Frey, which began, 'The agent of economic theory is rational, selfish, and his tastes do not change.' As Kahneman later put it: 'Here was an opportunity for an interesting conversation across the boundaries of disciplines.' That conversation became behavioural economics.

In a 1973 paper, co-written with Tversky, he coined a name for the tendency that he had recognised in his younger self to put too much faith in our power of judgement: 'the illusion of validity'. Their landmark 1974 *Science* article introduced three biases which affect our decision-making prowess. These were availability, anchoring, and representativeness.

One of the first to spot the connection with economics was Richard Thaler, who came across Kahneman and Tversky's *Science* paper in 1976 after a recommendation from a colleague. 'As I read, my heart started pounding the way it might during the final minutes of a close game. The paper took me thirty minutes to read from start to finish, but my life had changed forever.' Quite literally, it seems, Kahneman and Tversky were putting the feeling back into economics. The rest of this chapter looks at each of these heuristics in turn, starting with the most available.

Availability

The availability heuristic is simply the idea that we tend to go for whatever option, or information, seems the most convenient and accessible (such as the first on a list). Indeed, perhaps the most basic lesson of behavioural economics is that making decisions is hard, so we look for shortcuts. And we are easily influenced when someone – the state, an advertiser, our social group, or even our own habits – supplies that shortcut.

As an example, consider the vexed questions of what to eat for lunch, and when to eat it. According to the availability heuristic, we tend to take whatever option is closest to hand. One study by Yale School of Management and Google investigated the behaviour of people visiting Google's break rooms, which serve free drinks and snacks to employees. They found that visitors were 50 per cent more likely to grab a snack with their drink if the distance from snack station to beverage station was reduced from five metres to two metres. For men, they estimated that for just one visit per day, the total effect of all those extra snacks amounted in terms of weight gain to about a pound of fat per year.

Another way to exploit the availability heuristic is to provide convenient defaults, such as a suggested serving. The Google study found that when the most popular snack, M&Ms, was supplied in small, individual packages – instead of being self-served from bulk bins into cups – the average serving size reduced by 58 per cent, again with substantial effects on both the bottom line and the waistline.

According to the BBC, more than 150 governments around the world have adopted behavioural approaches. A leader in this area is Singapore, where 60 per cent of people eat at food courts four or more times a week. In recent years the country has collaborated with the UK's Nudge Unit to come up with schemes to promote public policies including healthy eating.

From a marketer's perspective the aim, of course, is usually to push people towards consuming more food, not less – and marketers are experts at using behavioural biases to influence us (and have been before they were called behavioural biases). Supermarkets position staples such as milk and eggs at the back of the store so that customers have to walk past all the tempting displays for more profitable (and possibly less healthy) items. They put pricey items at eye level where they are more likely to be noticed. And because making decisions is hard, they have learned to limit the number of options. In one experiment, when shoppers at a grocery store were offered a choice of 24 jams to taste, they ended up buying far less jam than when they only had a choice of six.

The easiest way to boost availability is through advertising. Marketers have long known that the best way to sell something is not to drown the consumer in information, it is to make their product look interesting or sexy or powerful, and prompt positive associations in the mind. If you show interest in buying something online, then ads for that item start trailing you as you browse the web, thanks to programs which track your every move. If an easily available story gets picked up by the media it can result in an 'availability cascade' where the story's accessibility means that it spreads in viral fashion.

Fortunately, if people abuse the free food at Google or otherwise end up eating too much junk, they can use behavioural economics to reduce their weight. The company stickK was started by Yale University professors Dean Karlan and Ian Ayres in 2007. Users select a goal, such as losing a certain amount of weight, and enter a contract where they agree to pay a certain amount, e.g. to a charity (or even an organisation they hate) if they fail to meet the goal.

Behavioural economics shows that people tend to be overly optimistic about their degree of control, so pick too ambitious a target. But on the other hand, loss aversion means that because they have skin in the game, they try harder. The combination of these two biases, working together, increases the chance that people lose weight. The company also uses the power of social norms to influence behaviour by creating an online network of friends and supporters, who can monitor your progress (ideally with text alerts sent out every time you eat an ice cream).

Finally, another kind of availability shortcut is provided by social norms, which act as a kind of rulebook that helps us make decisions. If most people around us think that lunch starts at 12.00, then we might feel uncomfortable eating before that hour. On the other hand, we are also affected more immediately by what others around us are doing – even when they are breaking the rules – in the phenomenon known as herd behaviour. The reason riots get started is exactly because people who otherwise would be rule-followers are encouraged by others to join the crowd. Less excitingly, if our friends are going for lunch, then we will too, even if we're not hungry.

In one recent collaboration between the media firm Kinetic UK and the 'behavioural interventions agency' Ogilvy Change, two different posters were placed around Lakeside Shopping Centre, Essex, in an attempt to modify shoppers' eating habits. In either case the copy was: 'Who says lunch has to be after 12? Food court open at 11.' The first poster featured a woman eating a hamburger, while the second showed a group sharing a pizza.

The experiment showed that the first poster increased food court footfall by 25 per cent, while the second poster – which tapped into herd behaviour – boosted it by 75 per cent. When people were asked afterwards why they had eaten early, they usually said it was because they were hungry – nothing to do with social norms or posters – showing that we tend to rationalise our responses. We will come back to social norms later, but the main point now is that we like to take shortcuts, be they physical, mental, or social. Especially when we are hungry.

Anchor aweigh

Next up in Kahneman and Tversky's 1974 list of cognitive biases was the anchoring heuristic. This refers to the idea that we tend to make decisions and estimates by making adjustments according to some reference point. The anchoring heuristic is related to the availability heuristic because in either case we are taking a kind of mental shortcut by opting for whatever option is closest, where here 'closest' is measured relative to our reference point.

Kahneman and Tversky illustrated their idea with an experiment in which one group of students was asked to estimate within five seconds the product $8 \times 7 \times 6 \times 5 \times 4 \times 3 \times 2 \times 1$ while another group did the same for the product $1 \times 2 \times 3 \times 4 \times 5 \times 6 \times 7 \times 8$. Since only the order of calculation is changed, the correct answer in either case is the same, namely 40,320. The median answer for the first group was 2,250, while for the second group it was 512. So, although both answers were wrong, the results seemed to indicate that the students were influenced by the order of the numbers, so their expectations were anchored by the magnitude of the first terms. If we see a price of £1599, we focus more on the 1500 than the 99 at the end.

Anchoring occurs with prices because while it is hard to estimate the cost of something, it is easy to measure changes in cost, so that is what we tend to focus on. An example is house prices. When we put a house up for sale, we will probably remember what we paid for it, but we may also have a more recent estimate based on sales of comparable properties. If house prices have risen sharply in recent years, then we will tend to anchor to the most recent such estimate. This is one reason why house prices tend to be 'sticky' on the way down.

For example, in 2017 the housing market in Vancouver, which had been booming for years, suddenly went into reverse. Demand fell off a cliff, but prices didn't immediately follow. As one prospective house-buyer told *The Globe and Mail*, 'Sellers are still in denial about the housing correction and unwilling to come down from that mythical price they have been banking on. Buyers, meanwhile, know the home is no longer worth what they are asking.'

In one study, researchers Greg Northcraft and Margaret Neale showed real estate agents a house, provided a list price, and asked them to estimate the appraisal value and purchase price. The agents' estimates were again affected by the list price, yet when questioned they denied that it had been a factor. For this reason the psychologist Adam Galinsky suggests that when selling a home, or making any kind of negotiation, it may make sense to start with a fairly aggressive price that acts as an anchor, but show flexibility.

Restaurants sometimes exploit the anchoring effect by including an obviously over-priced item on the menu. Customers anchor their prices to that level, and everything else seems quite reasonable. Retailers often use the 'list price' or 'suggested retail price' for the same reason, as a largely fictitious reference/anchor point to make it look like consumers are getting a good deal. Charities often suggest donation levels which act as an anchor and increase contributions.

False representation

The third type of heuristic considered by Kahneman and Tversky was representativeness. This refers to the fact that, when asked questions such as the probability that a person has a particular job, we tend to answer it by constructing a kind of story instead of by looking at the numbers.

For example, they performed a study where two groups of subjects were given personality profiles for several people, who they were told were randomly drawn from a list of 100 professionals. One group was told that the list consisted of 70 engineers and 30 lawyers, while the other was told that there were 30 engineers and 70 lawyers.

According to probability theory (Bayes' law), the chance that a person is in a particular group should scale with the relative size of the group. For example, if there were only one lawyer in the list and 99 engineers, then you would have to be pretty convinced by a personality profile to say that the person was definitely the lawyer. Doing the math shows that for a profile which doesn't fall neatly into one category over the other, one would expect the odds of being classified as an engineer to be higher for the first group (whose list supposedly contained 70 engineers) than the second (30 engineers) by a factor of more than five. In fact, though, the results were nearly identical. It seemed that the subjects were ignoring the numerical information and making their choice purely on how they imagined a person fitting into a particular group.

In a 1983 paper, Kahneman and Tversky provided an even more graphic illustration of the representativeness heuristic, in an experiment where they gave participants the following profile: 'Linda is 31 years old, single, outspoken, and very bright. She majored in philosophy. As a student, she was deeply concerned with issues of discrimination and social justice, and also participated in anti-nuclear demonstrations.' They then asked which was more probable: that (A) Linda is a bank teller, or (B) Linda is a bank teller and is active in the feminist movement.

The logically correct response for the 'Linda problem', as it became known, is (A), for the simple reason that the class includes all bank tellers, while (B) only includes those bank tellers who are feminists. The question is therefore like asking whether it is more likely that I roll a six, or that I roll a six while also drawing an Ace of Spades. Yet more than 80 per cent of participants chose (B). This tendency held even if the participants had a background in statistics.

According to the rule of conjunction in probability theory, the probability of two events occurring together must be less than or equal to the probability of either one occurring alone. The Linda problem is therefore an example of the 'conjunction fallacy' where we assign probabilities in a manner that doesn't agree with expected utility theory. We will see more of the conjunction fallacy in the next chapter.

Kahneman and Tversky argued that the reason we fall for things like the Linda effect is because we build up a mental representation of Linda, which we then attempt to fit with one of the available options. Linda's profile suggests someone who might be a feminist, so (B) appears to be the better match. It seems that we interpret information by making it fit with an available story. One reason we are susceptible to 'fake news' is that we favour information that backs up those stories. As we will see next, this desire to maintain a consistent story affects not just how we respond to things like surveys or advertisements, but how we experience reality in the first place.

Cognitive ease

Each of the three heuristics described by Kahneman and Tversky in their 1974 paper represents a mental shortcut that helps us to navigate the world. According to expected utility theory, we make decisions based on perfect information and perfect logic. The reality is that we tend to take whichever option presents itself first (availability), or serves as a benchmark (anchoring), or fits with our mental story (representativeness).

Kahneman and Tversky explained our reliance on heuristics by saying that we have two ways of thinking, which they dubbed System 1 and System 2. System 1, according to Kahneman, is 'fast, effortless, associative, and often emotionally charged'. It is also governed by habit, which makes it hard to change or control. System 2, in contrast, is 'conscious, it's deliberate; it's slower, serial, effortful, and deliberately controlled, but it can follow rules'.

In practice we tend to employ System 1 just because it is faster and requires less energy, but that means relying on rough-and-ready heuristics which are easily fooled, by marketers or by psychologists. One of the most basic lessons of statistics, for example, is that when estimating the frequency of an event, the accuracy depends on – and increases with – the size of the sample. This result, known as the Law of Large Numbers, was proved by the mathematician Jacob Bernoulli in 1713. But in their experiments, Kahneman and Tversky found an 'exaggerated confidence in the validity of conclusions based on small samples'. Their subjects consistently tended to 'view a sample randomly drawn from a population as highly representative, that is, similar to the population in all essential characteristics'. Again, this held even when the subjects were expert statisticians.

Heuristics are basically a way to save mental energy in the short term. The flip side of this is that we tend to reject information which doesn't fit with those biases, because to grapple with them is tiring. 'How do you know that a statement is true?' asks Kahneman in his 2011 book *Thinking, Fast and Slow*. 'If it is strongly linked by logic or association to other beliefs or preferences you hold, or comes from a source you trust and like, you will feel a sense of cognitive ease.'

Kahneman summed the problem up by saying that humans are 'blind to the obvious, and that we also are blind to our blindness'. As an illustration, he cited a famous experiment by psychologists Daniel Simons and Christopher Chabris, where subjects were asked to watch a short video of two teams – one in white shirts and the other in black shirts – each tossing a basketball around, and count how many times the white team pass their ball.

The gorilla in the room

The video has been viewed millions of times. If you have seen it, you'll know that you have to concentrate quite hard to get the answer right. If you haven't, then spoiler alert: in the middle of the video, a person in a gorilla suit walks in from the right, pauses to thump their chest, then walks off to the left. In the original experiment, about a half of the viewers failed to see the gorilla on the first viewing. A later experiment with eye-tracking found that some viewers even looked directly at the gorilla but still didn't see it.

In a way, this 'inattentional blindness', as it became known, seems stunning proof of our obliviousness. It has since been backed up by numerous other experiments – for example one where people walking down the street failed to notice a brightly coloured clown on a unicycle, especially if they were using a mobile phone (the respondents, not the clown; they also probably failed to notice other things, like lamp posts). London Transport did a version of the basketball video with a moonwalking man in a bear suit, as part of a bicycle safety campaign alerting car drivers to their lack of alertness.

A related phenomenon is change blindness. The difference here is that you do notice something, but you fail to realise that it has changed. In one experiment, a researcher stops someone to ask for directions. While they are talking, two people carrying a door walk between them – and, shielded by the door, one of them does a quick substitution with the first experimenter. In about 50 per cent of cases, the person being asked directions fails to notice that the person they are speaking with is different.

Inattentional blindness and change blindness are routinely exploited by magicians, and even made their way into the Official CIA Manual of Trickery and Deception. This was a document prepared for the CIA by the magician John Mulholland during the Cold War. Nuclear deterrence may have been based on rational game theory, but the CIA was ahead of the game at exploiting our cognitive shortcomings. Mulholland instructed spies on the dark arts of distraction, for example how raising a flaming match to a cigarette with one hand could distract a target's eyes from the drop of a poison pill into a drink with the other.

Active eye

While cognitive biases and heuristics often get a bad rap, we should point out that they have a useful side – indeed it would be hard to function without them. One reason is that, although expected utility theory assumes that we have infinite ability to observe and compute, our neural architecture is actually not quite up to that exalted standard. Consider, for example, the human eye.

The retina in the eye connects to the brain through the optic nerve. This consists of about a million neural wires called axons, each of which transmits one pixel of image. In terms of resolution, the eye is therefore the equivalent of a 1-megapixel camera. A high-end digital camera might have about twenty times that resolution.

The reason we aren't bothered by this lack of resolution is because our brain actively manages how we construct a mental image. The high-resolution part of the retina covers only about 1–2 degrees of vision. However, the eyes do not stay still like a camera lens, but take in a scene by making a sequence of tiny but extremely fast jerking motions called saccades, allowing the brain to build up a complete picture. When we pay attention to something, neurons in the brain's visual system increase activation (i.e. the firing rate) for that area but inhibit it elsewhere.

The process of observing a scene is therefore not a passive process, but is highly dynamic. In many ways the scene that we think we see is actually an illusion produced by the brain. When we concentrate on one area, we become insensitive or blind to another. It therefore isn't surprising that cognitive psychologists can devise experiments to trick the mind – especially since magicians have been doing the same thing for hundreds of years. More interesting is what this tells us about the way our minds work. Like our visual system, our brains have limitations, so place a frame around what they are interested in. But the placing of the frame is itself a creative act.

As Henry David Thoreau wrote in his 1862 book *Walden*, 'Objects are concealed from our view not so much because they are out of the course of our visual ray as because we do not bring our minds and eyes to bear on them.' This applies also in science: as Albert Einstein wrote in 1926: 'Whether you can observe a thing or not depends on the theory which you use. It is the theory which decides what can be observed.' Our perceptions are active constructions that represent our brain's guesses or predictions about the world.

While neoclassical economics treats us as omniscient beings, behavioural economics seems determined to show us up as frauds. But another approach, as the business professor Teppo Felin points out, is to focus on 'the role of human ingenuity in crafting questions, expectations, hypotheses and theories to make sense of their environments'. After all, the main difference between the human brain and a computer – even one equipped with a high-resolution digital camera – is that we know what we are looking for.

The gaze heuristic

As an example, consider the gaze heuristic, which is what we use when we are trying to position ourselves in order to catch a ball. If we were to program a robot to do this task, we might start by building an elaborate mathematical model which would take into account factors such as the ball's speed and position, air resistance, wind speed, and so on to calculate the ball's predicted trajectory. When we do it ourselves, we just use a simple heuristic, which is to move in such a way that our line of sight to the ball is maintained at a constant angle.

The result of this heuristic is that when the ball is launched into the air, we back away in order to lower the angle, and as it falls, we move closer. If the ball is going to one side, our path curves towards it. The heuristic isn't always perfect – for example, it tends to fail when a ball is hit straight up in the air – but it works well enough most of the time, which is why it is the go-to default for humans and dogs alike.

Of course, one could argue that it doesn't matter whether we use rational computations or simple heuristics if the end result in either case is that we catch the ball. In the same way, behavioural economics doesn't really question the neo-classical assumption that we are rational utility optimisers at heart, it only suggests that we make decisions subject to certain inherent limitations. Nor did behavioural economists challenge the assumption that human behaviour could be described and predicted by mathematics – it was just that economists needed a few more equations. The next chapter shows how this approach led to an alternative to expected utility theory known as prospect theory.

PROSPECT THEORY 4

As the behavioural approach to economics gained momentum, psychologists including Kahneman and Tversky added to the list of heuristics and biases first identified in their 1974 paper. Many of these seemed to be variants of one another. For example, status quo bias, which the Remain campaign attempted to evoke during the run-up to Brexit, seems to be related to the availability and anchoring heuristics, since the status quo is both available and serves as an anchor. Confirmation bias, where we interpret evidence to reinforce existing beliefs, and cognitive dissonance, which is a state of conflict between our beliefs and our actions, are related to representativeness, since in either case our perceptions are affected by the story we tell ourselves.

Science often proceeds through attempts to unify a range of disparate phenomena, and a step in this direction was taken with Kahneman and Tversky's prospect theory. This grew out of a technical report called 'Prospect Theory: An Analysis of Decision under Risk' that was written as part of the US Department of Defense's Advanced Decision

Technology Program. Their work was sponsored by the Defense Advanced Research Projects Agency (DARPA) which has been involved in the design of many key military technologies, including most famously the internet. The research was also monitored by the Office of Naval Research. An updated version of the theory was published in 1979 in the journal *Econometrica*, in an article with the same title.

Decision-making is obviously rather important for the military, and the report begins by noting that scientific interest in the area originated during the Second World War 'from the need to solve strategic and tactical problems in situations where experience was either costly or impossible to acquire'. The result was a 'technology for making decisions' whose validity relied on 'its underlying theoretical rationale'. However, while 'most students of the field regard the axioms of utility theory as canons of rational behavior', the reality was that actual decisions did not obey the said axioms. In other words, if utility theory was an instrument of war, then it didn't shoot straight.

The report then stated that 'Decision making under uncertainty can be viewed as a choice between gambles or prospects'. For simplicity, the authors restricted the discussion to 'gambles with (so called) objective probabilities'. The purpose of prospect theory was to express through mathematics how we make decisions about such prospects.

Of course, it should also be noted that in 1974 (and today) the government's interest in psychology didn't just extend to the nature of military decision-making. The CIA had just the year before wrapped up the infamous post-war MKUltra program, also known as the mind control program, whose remit included the study of techniques such as psychedelic drugs, hypnosis, and parapsychology. Cognitive approaches might have looked like another way to achieve the same aim. Behavioural science has always been as much about controlling decisions as about finding the best way to make them.

Place your bets

As a simple example of the kind of problem studied by Kahneman and Tversky, based on one in their paper, which of the following would you prefer:

A: £1,000 with probability 50%
£0 with probability 50%

or:

B: £450 with probability 100%

If we define u to be the individual's utility function, then the expected utility of option A is $u(1000) \times 0.5 + u(0) \times 0.5$, and the utility of option B is $u(450)$. If a person is 'risk neutral' then we can simply identify utility with the amount that is won or lost. A plot of utility versus price is just a straight line. In this case, option A is preferable since the utility is $u(1000) \times 0.5 + u(0) \times 0.5 = 1000 \times 0.5 + 0 \times 0.5 = 500$, while the utility of option B is only $u(450) = 450$. However, if a person is 'risk-averse' then they might choose the sure-thing option B instead. In order for this to happen mathematically, the utility function must be not a straight line as in the neutral case, but one that curves down (this is shown later in Figure 1 on page 62). A person who is risk-seeking, meanwhile, will have a utility function that curves up.

The idea that utility is a non-linear function of expected payout goes back to the eighteenth-century mathematician Daniel Bernoulli, who suggested that in psychological terms the utility (though he called it 'moral expectation') of money flattens out for larger amounts: a millionaire gets less joy from finding a ten-pound note in her coat pocket than does someone who is wondering where their next meal will come from. A salary increase from £20,000 to £30,000 has a bigger impact than one from £120,000 to £130,000. This behaviour is consistent with the axioms of expected utility theory. However, Kahneman and Tversky found a number of cases which violated these axioms, and drew the whole basis of the traditional theory into question.

Consider for example the following pair of games, again based on ones in their paper:

Game 3: choose between

A:	£40 with probability	80%
	£0 with probability	20%

and:

B:	£30 with probability	100%

Game 4: choose between

C:	£40 with probability	20%
	£0 with probability	80%

and:

D:	£30 with probability	25%
	£0 with probability	75%

The only difference between the games is that in Game 3 the probabilities of a win in each option are four times larger than the corresponding options for Game 4. In either case, the expected payout for the first option (A or C) is a little higher than for the second (B or D), so according to standard theory most people should choose that option. In experiments, though, most people chose option B for Game 3. The reason is that it represents a sure thing – and this turns out to be important.

Kahneman and Tversky interpreted this preference for certainty over uncertainty as an example of the certainty effect, also known as the Allais paradox, which was first described by the French economist Maurice Allais in 1952. It seems that the desire for an option with certainty interferes with and overrides our desire to choose the gamble with the best odds. In mathematical terms this means that we need to add appropriate weights to the components of the utility function, with a sure payout being weighted more heavily than one with uncertainty.

Loss aversion

Another problem with expected utility theory was that it treated losses and gains as equal but opposite in their effects on the human psyche; however, experiments revealed that our response to loss or gain is asymmetric. As an example, suppose you are offered the opportunity to bet on a single coin toss: heads you win $150, tails you lose $100. Would you take the gamble?

Most people would decline – and on average would need a potential win of $200 to balance the risk of loss (the 'loss aversion ratio' is usually in the range of 1.5 to 2.5). It seems that we fear loss more than we hope for gain. Neuroscientists have shown that the prospect of a loss is processed in the amygdala, which is the brain's centre for emotions such as fear and disgust.

One manifestation of loss aversion is the status quo bias, where we dislike change because it means losing what is familiar. As Kahneman wrote in 2011, 'loss aversion is a powerful conservative force that favors minimal changes from the status quo in the lives of both institutions and individuals. This conservatism helps keep us stable in our neighbourhood, our marriage, and our job; it is the gravitational force that holds our life together near the reference point.' (Though as David Cameron's Conservative Party discovered with the Brexit vote, this force can manifest itself in surprising ways.)

Loss aversion also plays a key role in decision-making by 'investors who evaluate a start-up, lawyers who consider whether to file a lawsuit, wartime generals who consider an offensive, and politicians who must decide whether to run for office'. Or as Kahneman and Tversky wrote more richly in their 1972 report, 'The greater sensitivity to negative rather than positive changes is not specific to monetary outcomes. It reflects a general property of the human organism as a pleasure machine.'

Loss aversion has an important influence over financial markets; the volume of trades is higher when prices are rising than when they are falling. The tendency to hold on to stocks that perform badly is common enough to get its own name, the 'disposition effect'. Sometimes this makes sense for tax purposes since the loss is deductible, but more often it is done in order to avoid acknowledging a bad investment decision.

The related 'sunk-cost fallacy' occurs when you put even more money into a poor investment in the hope that it will turn around and allow you to recoup your costs. If you have spent a lot of money on a pair of shoes that don't fit perfectly, then the pain of throwing them out might still be more than the pain of wearing them. The same can apply to a company's strategy – it would rather plough on as before, even if it's not working, rather than take the hit and go through the pain of revising its plans.

Like everything else, a sense of loss or regret depends on the context. For example, suppose that you considered making an investment in company X last year, but didn't. Shares of X went up by 25 per cent since then. You will feel a degree of regret. Now suppose that you had shares of company X last year, but decided to sell them. Objectively you are in the same place as in the first scenario – i.e. without shares in this great company – but you will almost certainly feel more regret, because the outcome was the result of an action on your part rather than the default which is inaction.

Sometimes we try to avoid future regret by avoiding action, or by staying with the safe default. For investment professionals, this usually means buying or selling when one's peers are doing the same, on the basis that an unusual decision will cause more regret in the case of a loss. And as John Maynard Keynes famously put it, 'Worldly wisdom teaches that it is better for reputation to fail conventionally than to succeed unconventionally.'

A related problem is that we may frame losses too narrowly. We might decline the coin toss bet, but if we were offered a hundred of them, we would be crazy not to accept, because the risk of losing shrinks to near-zero. Venture capital firms, for example, take bets on a portfolio of risky businesses in the hope that some will succeed, and more than compensate for the losses. A company with conservative managers, each of whom is assessing projects on an individual basis, may suffer from narrow framing and reject all risk, to the detriment of the company's long-term prospects.

Loss aversion is key to the science, or black arts, of marketing. Marketers often prefer to frame price promotions as a way to avoid loss, as when the reduction is billed as 'limited time only'. And companies spend a lot of money building a recognised brand in part because it represents reputational skin in the game – customers know that, unlike an unknown brand, a well-known company has a lot to lose if it delivers poor quality.

Finders keepers

Also related to loss aversion is the endowment effect, which is based on the empirical observation that people are willing to give up an item only at a price which is substantially more than they are willing to pay for it. This was illustrated in an experiment by Kahneman, Thaler, and Jack Knetsch, which Kahneman later described as 'the first application of prospect theory to an economic puzzle' and which 'now appears to have been a significant milestone in the development of behavioral economics'.

The researchers divided students into groups of buyers and sellers, where the object being bought or sold was a coffee mug, and asked them to come up with a reasonable price. The median selling price was $7.12 which was more than double the median buying price of $2.87. A number of experiments for different goods have shown that the ratio of buy/sell prices is typically around 2:1, as with the loss aversion ratio.

A similar effect is seen with typical household goods such as eggs or orange juice. Price changes do affect sales, as conventional theory expects, but the effect is not symmetric: price increases lower sales by about twice as much as price cuts raise them. The idea that gains and losses are experienced asymmetrically relative to a central reference point also helps to explain effects such as status quo bias. If change will have uncertain effects, then it is safer to stay at the reference point, since an equal probability of a negative result outweighs the same chance of a positive result.

Of course, people in the business of selling mugs do not feel this effect because they see the mugs as being held for exchange rather than for their own use. And for them, the outcome of a trade is viewed not as a one-off event, but as one trade in a long series. This 'broad framing' means that they focus more on the long-term profits. This is a useful lesson for investors, who will usually do much better if they avoid reacting to short-term fluctuations due to news, where loss aversion may cause them to make costly mistakes.

Ergodicity

While loss aversion is often framed as a kind of mental shortcoming that prevents us from reaching our full potential, in many cases it actually makes a lot of sense. The reason comes down to something that mathematicians call ergodicity.

Saying that a random process is ergodic means roughly that all of its statistics can be determined by taking a single long sample, so the future can be predicted by extrapolating from the past. For example, the risks run by a casino are ergodic because losses should be balanced by gains in the long run. However, for an individual gambler, risk is not ergodic, because a sequence of losses could wipe them out, so the game ends and there is no long run. What counts is not the average outcome, but the specific outcome for that person, which might be very different.

As another example, if a disease has a 1 per cent mortality rate, then on a population level 99 per cent will survive. On an individual level, you can't be 99 per cent alive – you are either alive or dead. The 1 per cent mortality rate therefore looms somewhat larger.

With something like an epidemic, fear of contagion may seem irrational on an individual basis. But as we will discuss in the final chapter, in relation to the COVID-19 crisis, epidemics in their early stage grow in an exponential fashion, not linearly. Taking low-cost precautions in the early stages is therefore the best approach. As Argentina's president Alberto Fernández said of his decision to impose an early lockdown, 'You can recover from a drop in the GDP. But you can't recover from death.'

Loss aversion also accounts for the fact that small risks accumulate in time. Smoking a single cigarette is not dangerous, but smoke a pack a day and it adds up. More generally, aversion to loss or uncertainty can reflect the fact that in real life the odds can never be precisely known, especially for rare events – and for all we know, the game might be rigged against us. So again, the average statistics don't apply, and we will only participate if there is some definite upside.

The value function

Kahneman and Tversky supplied many other examples where their respondents' answers to surveys and questionnaires didn't add up. The theory they developed to make sense of it all was based on two basic insights. 'One is the tendency for people to isolate a choice problem from their assets and evaluate it in terms of gains and losses.' What counts is not so much our total wealth, as Bernoulli had assumed, but changes relative to a reference point, such as an anchor price or the status quo (if we are expecting a certain raise in salary, then anything smaller will come as a disappointment). Our sensitivity to change is proportional to the amount of change, but there is also a saturation effect for large changes.

The second insight involved 'the replacement of sub-jective possibilities by uncertainty weights which reflect attitudes toward uncertainty and not merely degrees of belief'. In other words, our response does depend on our preferences, just as expected utility theory assumes – it is just that these preferences now include our attitudes towards different types of risk. As we'll see, in framing the question this way, and mathematicising the results, Kahneman and Tversky laid out the path which behavioural economics would follow until the present day.

Kahneman and Tversky summed up their insight that losses and gains are handled differently with a sketch like the one shown in Figure 1, overleaf. The horizontal axis shows monetary loss or gain, relative to a central reference point at the origin. The vertical axis shows psychological value. In the upper right quadrant, value rises with gains, but curves down. This reflects the saturation effect, where we value gains less as we accumulate more. The lower left quadrant shows how monetary losses are perceived. The shape here is similar, but the slope of the line near the origin is steeper, which reflects the fact that we are more sensitive to losses than to gains, and the line curves up, which reflects saturation with respect to losses.

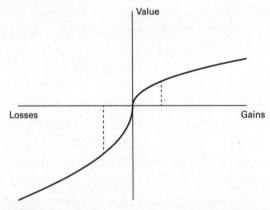

Figure 1. Plot of a value function. The exact shape of the curve will be different for different people.

In addition to the value function, Kahneman and Tversky introduced a weighting function for uncertainty, denoted by the symbol π (see Figure 2). This function represents not a subjective probability but rather the willingness to gamble on an event. For the games discussed above, the function π was assumed to be the same as the probability.

The main role of the uncertainty weighting was to account for the observed tendency of people to overreact to small probability events. For example, tourists visiting a city after a recent terrorist attack may worry about being killed in such an attack more than about the much likelier chance of being run over by a car. In part this is because of the availability heuristic – terrorists are experts at seeding fear in a population – but it is also because we tend to over-weight low-probability events.

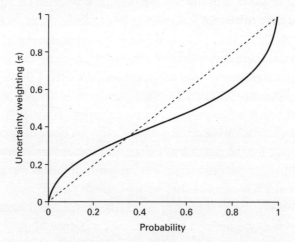

Figure 2. Plot of an uncertainty weighting function. The curve will be different for losses and gains, but similar in shape, and again will vary between people.

Note that the slope of the graph is steepest for probabilities near 0 and 1. This reflects the certainty effect discussed above (see page 55) and also the 'possibility effect'. Suppose you are told that the possibility of you winning £1 million increases:

A. From 0 to 5 per cent
B. From 50 to 55 per cent
C. From 95 to 100 per cent

Option A is exciting because it means going from 0 to having a shot at winning a huge prize: the possibility effect.

According to expected utility theory, the appropriate weights are just the probabilities on a scale of 0 to 1, so 0.0 and 0.05. However, if we treat Figure 2 as representative of this scenario, we see that the actual weights are 0.0 and 0.13, so the possibility of winning something has a much higher weight.

Option C is exciting too because it includes the possibility of a sure thing: the certainty effect. In expected utility theory, the appropriate weights are 0.95 and 1.0; on the curve they are 0.79 and 1.0. So, again, there is a much bigger boost between the two.

Industries have sprung up to cater to both of these – lotteries for the possibility effect, and insurance or annuity schemes for the certainty effect. In terms of thrills, the loser is B, which seems like just an adjustment to the prize.

Finally, while most people are risk-averse when it comes to profits (we prefer a sure gain over a chance of one) that changes when it comes to losses. Consider for example the following pair of games, where the minus sign indicates a loss.

Game 5: choose between gains

> A: £40 with probability   80%
>   £0 with probability   20%

or

> B: £30 with probability   100%

Game 6: choose between losses

> C: –£40 with probability   80%
>   –£0 with probability   20%

or

D: −£30 with probability   100%

Here a risk-averse player might be expected to select the sure-thing options of B in Game 5 and D in Game 6. However, the experimental results showed that most respondents choose the safe option B in Game 1, but the risky option C in Game 2. It seems that we are willing to spin the wheel in order to reduce risk. This is consistent with the idea that losses saturate in the same way as gains do – the possibility of a larger loss gets less of a psychological weight.

The fourfold way

Kahneman and Tversky summarised some of the key findings of prospect theory in the 'fourfold pattern'. This sketches four scenarios that capture the behaviour and interaction of the value function and uncertainty function, and according to Kahneman 'is considered one of the core achievements of prospect theory'.

	WIN £10K	LOSE £10K
Possibility effect – low chance	5% chance to win – risk-seeking, hope of gain, buy lottery ticket	5% chance to lose – risk-averse, fear of loss, buy insurance
Certainty effect – high chance	95% chance to win – risk-averse, fear of missed gain, be conservative	95% chance to lose – risk-seeking, hope to avoid loss, take a chance

These effects apply differently depending on whether you expect to win or lose. Consider a legal case which the plaintiff has an excellent 95 per cent chance of winning (see lower row). She will be risk-averse and may be tempted to accept a settlement for 90 per cent of the full claim. The defendant, however, expects to lose so will be risk-seeking and is unlikely to accept a settlement. This puts them in a less flexible bargaining stance, which is why such settlements tend to favour the defendant. On the other hand, frivolous litigation lives in the top row: the plaintiff is risk-seeking, while now the defendant is risk-averse.

Outside of law courts, the dangerous scenario is often the one in the bottom right cell, where when faced with a loss we are tempted to take a risk instead of accepting the hit. We also have particular problems with probabilities that are extremely low (smaller than 1 per cent) or very high (greater than 99 per cent). Either we ignore them completely, or we tend to overweight them – as with scare stories, where some risk factor is ignored by everyone until it suddenly gets blown up by the media in an availability cascade.

We are also sensitive to the way the risk is presented. If a chemical carries a 0.0001 per cent risk of causing cancer, that sounds pretty small. If we are told the chemical causes cancer in 1 out of every 100,000 people exposed to it, then we focus on that one person, and tend to overweight the risk. So if a company wants to hide a risk, it will go with the percentage, but if an advocacy group or a lawyer wants to highlight it, it will describe people affected. As we saw earlier, in the run-up to Brexit, the Leavers' claim that membership of the EU cost £350 million per week loomed much larger than the Chancellor's estimate cost for leaving of £4,300 per household per year, even though it worked out to a smaller amount.

Finally, Kahneman and Tversky included in their prospect theory an initial editing stage, in which respondents carried out a preliminary analysis of the offered prospects. Most of this consisted of basic simplifications, such as calibrating prospects according to the reference point, translating different outcomes to losses or gains, rounding numbers, and omitting factors that are common to all the prospects or seem extraneous. As we will see next, though, this editing can be less of a copyedit, and more like a complete rewrite.

'PARADOXES'

5

The original version of prospect theory did a lot to make sense of the heuristics and biases identified by psychologists that could be viewed as what Kahneman called the 'operating characteristics of System 1'. By adjusting the value and uncertainty curves appropriately, the resulting behavioural model could be used to fit experimental results. One of the theory's main achievements was to show how economic decisions are not taken in a vacuum, but depend on history and context. At the same time, while the model was becoming more flexible and realistic, it was also losing its simplicity and elegance.

In mathematical modelling, it is preferable to have a simple model that explains a lot and can be used to make predictions, as opposed to a complicated model that can fit anything but is unreliable for predictions. One measure of a model's complexity is the number of parameters that need to be adjusted. A straight line is a paradigmatic example of a simple model because it involves only two parameters, the slope and the intercept. If the line goes through the origin then the intercept is zero and the only parameter is the slope. In expected utility theory, for a risk-neutral person, the value function for a lottery is just the expected pay-off, so a straight line through the origin. For a risk-averse person, there is an additional parameter which controls the degree of saturation. Again, this saturation reflects our tendency to experience gains or losses at a proportionally lower rate as they increase in magnitude, and in graphical terms corresponds to a flattening of the value function curve. The uncertainty, meanwhile, is just the unadjusted probability.

Prospect theory provided greater realism at the expense of extra parameters. The value function was now asymmetric around the origin, so the slope and the saturation were different for gains and losses. The position of the reference point was also not clearly defined, and could be influenced by things like context. The uncertainty weighting function added an extra layer of complexity by overweighting low probabilities.

As Kahneman and Tversky wrote, 'The simultaneous measurement of values and decision weights involves serious experimental and statistical difficulties.' The model was therefore better seen as a descriptive tool rather than a reliably predictive one.

And the model still had a few glitches. For example, it couldn't easily be extended to prospects with many possible outcomes. It also only dealt with games where the probabilities of the different outcomes were known exactly. Any decision involves putting weights (usually subconsciously) on the likelihood and attractiveness of different possible outcomes, and an advantage of using gambles is that the probabilities at least can be calculated, which makes it easy to spot our cognitive errors. In most real-life situations, however, we deal not with probabilities, but with uncertainties, which is not the same thing. In a casino we can estimate the outcome of a roulette wheel probabilistically, but in the real world, things aren't that neat. In this chapter, we show how prospect theory was challenged by a number of 'paradoxes' which seem to elude even adjusted versions of classical logic.

The Ellsberg paradox

One way to handle cases where the exact odds are not known, as argued by the mathematician Leonard Savage in his 1954 *Foundations of Statistics*, is to replace the objective probabilities of expected utility theory with subjective probabilities of the decision-maker, which will be different for different people. However, while this conflation of uncertainty with probability is the standard approach in economics, it opens up another area for confusion, as illustrated in an experiment proposed and popularised by Daniel Ellsberg.

Ellsberg was a military analyst who spent his early career doing nuclear war planning for the US government at RAND, and famously leaked the Pentagon Papers – a top-secret study of US involvement in the Vietnam War – to the press in 1971. Ellsberg had done his PhD in risk analysis, and one of the experiments he studied involved the following game. An urn contains 90 balls, of which 30 are red and 60 are an unknown mix of black and yellow. You are given the choice between two gambles for a draw of a single ball.

In Game 1, you bet on drawing either red or black.

In Game 2, you bet on drawing red or yellow, or black or yellow.

Which would you prefer?

In each game, given that there are three colours and there is no reason to think that one is more likely than the other, the chances of drawing a red, black or yellow ball are indistinguishable. The only difference between the games is that in Game 2, each side of the bet includes yellow. So, if you prefer red in Game 1, then you should prefer 'red or yellow' in Game 2. However, most people see it differently – they don't look at the colour of the ball, but at the uncertainty.

In Game 1, the number of red balls is known to be 30, but the number of black balls is uncertain. They therefore choose red in Game 1. In Game 2, the number of yellow balls is uncertain; however, the sum of black and yellow balls is known to be 60. They therefore choose to bet on 'black or yellow', since again that is the option with less uncertainty.

This behavioural effect is known as ambiguity aversion. The inconsistency contradicts expected utility theory, but it also can't be treated by adjusting the probability weights, as in prospect theory, for the simple reason that we don't know the probabilities.

Our dislike of ambiguity was also demonstrated in the Nixon tapes, where President Nixon's Chief of Staff Harry Haldeman explained to Nixon that the problem with the Pentagon Papers was that they show that 'people do things the president wants to do even though it's wrong, and the president can be wrong'. We want to put faith in our leaders, rather than deal with difficult ambiguities.

Sure thing

The Ellsberg paradox involves a violation of something known as the sure thing principle, which states that if a person will make a certain decision if an event has occurred, and also if the event does not occur, then information about the event has no bearing on their decision.

The sure thing principle was illustrated by Savage using the following story. 'A businessman contemplates buying a certain piece of property. He considers the outcome of the next presidential election relevant. So, to clarify the matter to himself, he asks whether he would buy if he knew that the Democratic candidate were going to win, and decides that he would. Similarly, he considers whether he would buy if he knew that the Republican candidate were going to win, and again finds that he would.' He therefore goes ahead and buys.

While the principle sounds obvious, in fact we break it all the time – which is a problem because it violates the classical laws of probability. In the Ellsberg paradox, the difference between the games is information about the number of yellow balls. Since the number appears on both sides of the bet, this information shouldn't make any difference, but in practice it does.

The difference between judging probabilities and dealing with ambiguities has been demonstrated by neuroscientists. Behavioural economist Colin Camerer and colleagues, for example, carried out a version of the Ellsberg experiment, using cards instead of balls, on subjects while their brains were being scanned by an MRI machine, and found that the brain responds in quite different ways to the problems, even though they are really the same. They then repeated the experiment on five patients where the relevant areas had been damaged by stroke or other injuries – and found that they responded in the logical manner. In this case at least, it seems that the closest thing to rational economic man may be someone with brain damage.

As Camerer pointed out, ambiguity aversion could explain the phenomenon of home bias, where investors tend to invest mostly in their own country and are reluctant to stray too far afield. 'People tend to be way over-invested in their own country's stock. If you're in Brazil or Sweden, you're way under-diversified.'

A related effect is source-dependence, where a person's tolerance for uncertainty varies with its source, so for example people prefer to bet on their own judgement rather than someone else's. As with risk-tolerance, our attitude towards ambiguity is context-dependent. One study showed that there is a crossover point where investment managers become ambiguity-seeking as the probability of a loss increases, and fear is replaced by hope. Similarly, as the probability of a gain increases, hope may cross over to fear.

Do you want to play again?

In Chapter 3 we discussed the conjunction fallacy, which refers to our tendency to assume that a specific scenario (Linda is a feminist AND a bank teller) is more likely than a general one (Linda is a bank teller). We can also offer the disjunction fallacy, which involves the word OR.

Tversky, together with behavioural scientist Eldar Shafir, provided an example in an experiment with students involving a two-stage gamble. The students were first asked to decide on a gamble that offers an equal chance of winning $200 or losing $100. Some at random were then told that they had won the gamble; another group were told they had lost; and a third were not told the outcome. Then they were asked if they would like to play again. The results showed 'yes' for 69 per cent of those told they had won, and 59 per cent of those told they had lost – but only 36 per cent of those who didn't know. So being told you have won, or told you have lost, beats being told nothing – which doesn't make sense, since you must have either won or lost.

Tversky and Shafir also tried the following version:

Imagine that you have just taken a tough qualifying examination. It is the end of the fall quarter, you feel tired and run-down, and you are not sure that you passed the exam. In case you failed you have to take the exam again in a couple of months – after the Christmas holidays. You now have an opportunity to buy a very attractive 5-day Christmas vacation package in Hawaii at an exceptionally low price. The special offer expires tomorrow, while the exam grade will not be available until the following day. Would you:

(a) buy the vacation package.

(b) not buy the vacation package.

(c) pay a $5 non-refundable fee in order to retain the rights to buy the vacation package at the same exceptional price the day after tomorrow – after you find out whether or not you passed the exam.

In this version, 32 per cent chose option (a), 7 per cent option (b), and a majority of 61 per cent went for option (c). These results can be compared with a second version of the experiment which had exactly the same rules, except that now the students were told whether they had passed the exam or not, using the wording in round brackets in the former case and the wording in square brackets in the latter case.

> Imagine that you have just taken a tough qualifying examination. It is the end of the fall quarter, you feel tired and run-down, and you find out that you (passed the exam) [failed the exam. You will have to take it again in a couple of months – after the Christmas holidays]. You now have an opportunity to buy a very attractive 5-day Christmas vacation package to Hawaii at an exceptionally low price. The special offer expires tomorrow. Would you:
>
> (a) buy the vacation package
>
> (b) not buy the vacation package
>
> (c) pay a $5 non-refundable fee in order to retain the rights to buy the vacation package at the same exceptional price the day after tomorrow.

In this case more than half the students chose to buy the vacation package if they knew the outcome, whether it was pass (54 per cent chose to buy) or fail (57 per cent). This compares with the 32 per cent who chose to buy the package if they didn't know the outcome. It seems that, rather than adding together in a classical manner, reasons for action – in this case, knowing that you passed, or knowing that you failed – can interfere and cancel out. We return to this topic in the final chapter.

Tversky and Shafir concluded that the presence of ambiguity 'tends to blur the picture and makes it harder for people to see through the implications of each outcome'.

It also blurs the application of prospect theory, which deals with known risks rather than fuzzy uncertainties.

You've been framed

Another complexity with prospect theory is that outcomes are measured according to a central reference point, and the fact that we respond to losses and gains in an asymmetric way means that we can be easily influenced by the way that a problem is posed. The reference point is affected by a kind of inertia but is not set in stone, and an outcome might be viewed as a gain or a loss depending on the exact context.

In a 1981 paper called 'The Framing of Decisions and the Psychology of Choice', Kahneman and Tversky reported results for an experiment where respondents were given the following scenario. The US is preparing for an outbreak of an unusual disease which is predicted to kill 600 people if left untreated. 'Two alternative programs to combat the disease have been proposed. Assume that the exact scientific estimate of the consequences of the programs are as follows: If Program A is adopted, 200 people will be saved. If Program B is adopted, there is ⅓ probability that 600 people will be saved, and ⅔ probability that no people will be saved.' Again, in real life the outcomes of an unusual disease outbreak are unknown, but let's go with the game.

For this scenario, it turns out that most people are risk-averse: 78 per cent chose the certain prospect A of saving 200 lives. However, a second group was given an alternative scenario. In Program C 400 people will die. In Program D there is a ⅓ probability that nobody will die, and ⅔ probability that 600 people will die. Here the response was the mirror image, with most people choosing the riskier prospect D.

This fits the pattern that people are risk-averse in gains and risk-seeking in losses. But here the two scenarios are actually the same – the only difference is that the first is expressed in terms of gains, and the second in terms of losses.

Of course, marketers and advertisers have long known that we respond to information differently depending on the way that it is presented. An example reported by Richard Thaler was that credit card companies always insisted that any surcharge on credit cards was framed as a discount on cash rather than a surcharge on credit cards. That way, if a retailer imposed a surcharge, someone using a credit card would not perceive it as a direct loss. According to Kahneman, 'The concept of loss aversion is certainly the most significant contribution of psychology to behavioral economics. This is odd, because the idea that people evaluate many outcomes as gains or losses, and that losses loom larger than gains, surprises no one.' The difference is that behavioural economists came up with a mathematical model for it.

Another framing effect occurs because saturation effects depend on how a situation is judged relative to the reference point. As an illustration, Kahneman and Tversky used the following problem, where one group of respondents was told the prices in round brackets, and the other group the ones in square brackets.

Imagine that you are about to purchase a jacket for ($125) [$15], and a calculator for ($15) [$125]. The calculator salesman informs you that the calculator you wish to buy is on sale for ($10) [$120] at the other branch of the store, located 20 minutes' drive away. Would you make the trip to the other store?

Each group therefore has an opportunity to save $5, the only difference is in the framing. In the experiment, 68 per cent would make the trip to save $5 on a $15 calculator but only 29 per cent would do so to save $5 on a $125 calculator. The reason is that the value function saturates at larger values, so when the saving is judged relative to a higher price, it seems smaller.

More generally, framing occurs because we adjust and calibrate information in order to make it fit our mental model of reality. A graphic illustration of the framing effect was provided by the 2007–8 financial crisis, which grew out of an unfolding and very visible mortgage crisis in the US. As behavioural economists George Akerlof and Robert Shiller wrote in their 2015 *Phishing for Phools*: 'It is truly remarkable that so few economists foresaw what would happen.' They ascribed this to the 'mental frame' of economists which sees markets as fundamentally efficient, and blames pathologies on externalities. As with the gorilla experiment, we will ignore information if it doesn't mesh easily with our mental model.

Mental accounting

Just as framing can affect the reference point we use for assessing losses and gains, so can a kind of internal framing, in the form of mental accounting.

As an example, imagine that you have decided to see a movie which costs £10. As you enter the line for the box office you discover that you lost a £10 note. Would you still go ahead and buy a ticket? Most people say yes (in one experiment, 88 per cent). Now imagine that you discover you lost, not the money, but the ticket you purchased earlier. Would you buy another ticket now? In the experiment, only 46 per cent said they would, even though in monetary terms the two are equivalent. The reason is that we keep separate mental accounts. In the second scenario, it seems we are paying £20 to see a film, which seems excessive. In the first scenario, the loss comes out of our mental equivalent of a general cash account.

Mental accounting can be useful because it can act as a kind of savings device. For example, we treat money differently if it has been set aside for a goal such as retirement or making a special purchase. But it can also lead to expensive mistakes. As we will see later, financial markets do a good job of bringing out all of our behavioural biases. A well-known phenomenon is that people prefer to sell stocks that have done well, over ones that have lost money. This is due to a number of factors, but one is that, if a stock has gone up in value, then the profit seems like play money – or what a gambler would call 'house money' – so it is easier to spend on something else. Money realised from selling an investment that has gone down in value feels more like crystallising a painful loss. Ideally, of course, the investor should keep whichever assets seem most likely to rise in the future, which is a completely different question.

Our tendency to create separate accounts also influences our behaviour in other ways that often confound conventional models. One side effect of the financial crisis was that in 2008, US gasoline prices approximately halved. Consumers reacted by suddenly developing a preference for more expensive 'premium' gasoline, since their fuel budget could now afford it, rather than spending their savings on something else.

An experiment led by Colin Camerer analysed trip data for New York City cab drivers. Rather than driving as much as possible during busy periods, and taking a break at times when there was less demand as conventional theory would predict, drivers were doing the opposite: they would work until a certain target amount was achieved, which would take less time on busy days and more time on quiet days. Camerer and his colleagues suggested that drivers were using the target as a form of pre-commitment, which ensured they earned a steady income and weren't tempted to slack off. We discuss the issue of self-control further in the next chapter.

Preference reversal

Another aspect of human behaviour which confounds both classical utility theory and prospect theory is the phenomenon of preference reversal – otherwise known as changing your mind. In a 1971 paper called 'Reversals of preference between bids and choices in gambling decisions', psychologists Sarah Lichtenstein and Paul Slovic conducted an experiment where subjects were offered two bets similar to the following. A roulette wheel with 36 sectors will be spun. The options are:

A. 11 of the 36 sectors give a win of £160, 25 of 36 lose £15
B. 35 of the 36 sectors give a win of £40, 1 of 36 lose £10

The expected win for A is $^{11}/_{36} \times 160 - {^{25}/_{36}} \times 15 = £38.47$, while that for B is $^{35}/_{36} \times 40 - {^{1}/_{36}} \times 10 = £38.61$, which is nearly identical. Most people preferred B because it is less risky. But people were then asked how much they would charge if selling tickets for these bets to another person. This time they ranked A as being the better (so more expensive) bet, probably because they focused on the possibility of the larger prize. However, from the standpoint of classical theory this is confusing, because nothing about the problem itself has changed.

This preference reversal was in fact one of the first results from experimental psychology to win a degree of attention from economists. In a 1979 article two economists, David Grether and Charles Plott, responded by acknowledging that such effects are not only inconsistent with expected utility theory, but imply that 'no optimization principles of any sort lie behind even the simplest of human choices'. However they also pointed out that just because classical theory is 'subject to exception' does not mean it should be discarded, especially since 'No alternative theory currently available appears to be capable of covering the same extremely broad range of phenomena'. Indeed, as Kahneman later noted, the paper had 'little direct effect on the convictions of economists'.

Of course, we have already seen many examples where context or the framing of a problem changes the way we see it; and Tversky and Kahneman argued in a 1990 paper that preference reversal can be explained using prospect theory, by saying that the change of context forces subjects to switch from System 1 to System 2 thinking. When choosing the bet for themselves, they are affected by System 1 effects such as risk aversion: they prefer to go with game B because it is safer. When pricing the game, they put on their System 2 hat and do the math, so select game A.

However, while preference reversal can be explained this way, it also points to a fundamental flaw in the theory. The main results of prospect theory are captured by Figures 1 and 2 above (pages 62–3), which showed the value function and the uncertainty function. These functions already incorporate a mix of System 1 and System 2 attributes, of rationality (the functions are almost linear) and irrationality (they depart from linearity in places). But to explain preference reversal, we need to include a complete switch from one way of thinking to another, in a manner that depends only on context, rather than the nature of the problem. The phenomenon therefore seems to elude treatment using a mathematical model.

In the classical picture, experiments such as gambles are a way to reveal a person's true preferences. But, as suggested by the name, preference reversal implies that the preferences themselves are not constant. Instead they are, in a sense, made up in response to a question, as part of what Tversky and Thaler called 'a constructive, context-dependent process'. And viewed this way, questions are not just a passive way to elicit preferences – they actually affect those preferences. The measurement changes what is being measured. We return to this topic in the final chapter.

Primed

Another cognitive effect, related to framing, is the concept of priming. Instead of depending directly on how a scenario is presented, priming occurs when seeds are planted in a person's mind, which affects their perception in subtle ways. In his 2011 book *Thinking, Fast and Slow*, Kahneman reported a number of experimental studies which seemed to back up the power of priming.

One of these was the 'Florida effect' experiment in which 30 students were asked to solve a problem which involved unscrambling a number of words. For one group, the puzzle used words associated with elderliness such as 'Florida' or 'Bingo' while the second didn't. The students were timed as they left the laboratory to see how quickly they walked. According to the experimenters, the students who had been primed to think about old people walked more slowly.

One of the most effective priming devices turned out to be money. Participants exposed to words or cues related to money – such as computer with a screensaver showing floating dollar bills – behaved in a way that was more independent and selfish. For example, they were less likely to help other students with problems, and chose to sit further away from one another. The same effect appears when people are asked to think about economics or finance. Perhaps the most insidious effect of rational economic man is that it acts as a role model for students, and primes us to act in a particular way. As economist Kate Raworth wrote in 2017, rational economic man 'is the protagonist in every mainstream economics textbook; he informs policy decision-making worldwide; he shapes the way we talk about ourselves; and he wordlessly tells us how to behave.'

Another effective primer was pictures of eyes. An experiment where pictures of eyes or flowers were placed above an 'honesty box' taking payments for milk showed that the eyes picture resulted in far higher payments. Given the priming power of money and eyes, it is perhaps concerning that the US dollar bill has a picture of an all-seeing eye on the back of it.

In *Thinking, Fast and Slow* Kahneman pointed out that however unlikely it might seem that we can be so easily influenced, 'disbelief is not an option. The results are not made up, nor are they statistical flukes. You have no choice but to accept that the major conclusions of these studies are true. More important, you must accept that they are true about *you*.' We return to this assertion, and the question of priming, below.

The choice architects

Kahneman and Tversky developed a more refined version of prospect theory in a 1992 paper, which tidied up the mathematics and included scope for uncertainty. However, it could only partially address the central problem that, while one can plot probabilities on a graph, uncertainties usually resist precise quantification. In the Ellsberg paradox, for example, it is known that the numbers of black and yellow balls add up to 60, but in real life we often have no idea even what the possibilities are, let alone the probabilities.

The theory also assumed that pay-offs can be expressed numerically, while again, in real life, not every question can be quantified (e.g. whom to marry). And the phenomenon of preference reversal showed that weighting of preferences wasn't always enough, since the preferences themselves can change. Other behaviours including the conjunction fallacy, the disjunction fallacy, order effects (where our response depends on the order in which questions are asked, as we will discuss later), and so on could not be handled by prospect theory so required separate treatment.

Even with these drawbacks, it was clear that prospect

theory had immediate applications in economics and other areas such as law and politics – not just by helping to understand human behaviour, but by providing ways to control it. All you needed to do was control the context.

Thaler and law professor Sunstein defined a 'choice architecture' as the way in which a set of choices is presented, for example the physical layout, descriptive text or images, the presence of a default option, and so on. Anyone from a cafeteria manager to a doctor describing treatment options to a patient, to an architect optimising the layout of a building, to the person selecting the correct wording for a referendum question, is a choice architect. A 'nudge' is 'any aspect of the choice architecture that alters people's behavior in a predictable way without forbidding any options or significantly changing their economic incentives'. The use of such nudges to improve people's lives (as opposed to e.g. just selling them more stuff) is called 'libertarian paternalism'. As mentioned earlier, this approach became influential with governments around the world during the early 2000s.

Man versus machine

In many respects, prospect theory seemed to represent a fundamental challenge to the neoclassical model. At the same time, it didn't depart greatly from the 'normative' view of rationality, meaning that rationality was still held up as a kind of reference point for human behaviour, if only as an aspirational goal. Instead of rational economic man, we had a creature who tried to behave rationally, and even *thought* he was behaving rationally, but fell short due to various cognitive shortcomings.

One consequence was that our foibles came across in a rather negative light. Thaler and Sunstein, for example, wrote that 'people tend to be somewhat mindless, passive decision makers'. As prospect theory states, however, our impressions – including for things like economic theories – are relative to a reference point. If the reference point is taken as rational economic man, then the only competition for that would be a computer, which seems to be an argument for algorithms using artificial intelligence. Indeed, Daniel Kahneman told an audience in Toronto in 2017 that 'You should replace humans by algorithms whenever possible, and this is really happening. Even when the algorithms don't do very well, humans do so poorly and are so noisy that just by removing the noise you can do better than people.'

However, while prospect theory has been very successful at identifying and explaining our departures from rationality, it succeeds in part because of the careful way that it frames the problem. As Kahneman and Tversky wrote in 1981: 'For simplicity, we restrict the formal treatment of the theory to choices involving stated numerical probabilities and quantitative outcomes, such as money, time, or number of lives.' Furthermore, uncertainties could be expressed mathematically in terms of probabilities. And in all cases, there was a well-defined notion of what the rational person (or robot) would do. As mentioned above, though, most real-world problems aren't so neat. One could argue that being very good at solving narrow probabilistic problems might be maladaptive if it interferes with the ability to cope with complex, fast-moving scenarios of the kind we encounter in our daily lives. In the next chapter, we show how factors such as personality and emotions affect our decisions, in a way which is not easily captured by classical equations.

Fake news

Before proceeding, though, let's go back to the topic of priming, and how context affects impressions. As Kahneman observed, we tend to accept something as true if it comes from an apparently trustworthy source. However some readers – particularly those of a number-crunching System 2 bent – may have bristled a little at the statement that they 'have no choice but to accept' the conclusions of behavioural psychologists when it comes to things like priming. And some may even have thought that for a statistical study purporting to prove a rather unlikely phenomenon such as the 'Florida effect' the sample size of 30 students seemed a little small. After all, as behavioural psychologists are fond of pointing out, a common error is to make conclusions based on small samples. And do people start walking with a limp when they pass a retirement home? Surely an experimenter would want to confirm the result using a larger sample?

However, this is not what happened – at least until 2012, so some sixteen years after the original study, when a group of researchers went to the trouble of trying to replicate the result through two experiments.

The first experiment, on students, showed that the 'Florida effect' was not reproduced. The second, on researchers, showed that the effect did exist – for experimenters. If they were primed to believe the effect was real, then it affected their measurements – the students were recorded as walking more slowly when primed. In other words, priming seemed to be real, but not quite in the way advertised. (Perhaps another experiment will show that these experiments were themselves influence by priming, and so on.)

Kahneman quickly distanced himself from the research

on priming, writing an open letter to people in the field: 'I am not a member of your community, and all I have personally at stake is that I recently wrote a book that emphasizes priming research as a new approach to the study of associative memory – the core of what dual system theorists call System 1.' However, he warned that 'I see a train wreck looming. I expect the first victims to be young people on the job market. Being associated with a controversial and suspicious field will put them at a severe disadvantage in the competition for positions.' After all, other areas of psychology had fallen into 'a prolonged eclipse after similar outsider attacks on the replicability of findings'. This was a reference to the so-called replicability crisis, in which many published results in a range of areas including psychology and biology were found to not hold up after repeated testing.

Sample size is obviously a concern in an area like behavioural economics, where most of the experimental results used to develop things like prospect theory were based on questionnaires sent to a rather small sample (ranging usually from a few tens to a few hundreds) of predominately WEIRD students (Western, educated, and from industrialised, rich, and democratic countries). Another problem for all areas of scientific research is that incentives point towards finding positive results. An experiment which fails to provide an interesting conclusion won't be published – but if you perform many experiments, then some of them will give an interesting-looking result just by chance, and those are the ones that get selected for publication. If the paper is published by a trusted and credible source, then other researchers often fall in line and unconsciously make their data agree with it.

An early example of this phenomenon was when the eminent zoologist Theophilus Painter published a paper in

1921 which announced that, using a microscope, he had counted the number of human chromosomes, and there were 24 pairs. Other scientists repeated his observations, and also came up with 24. Some 30 years later, new methods were developed in which cells were fixed on microscope slides, thus enabling better observations – of 23 pairs. However, textbooks from the time showed photographs of chromosomes in which there were clearly 23, and yet the caption said there were 24. In other words, the results could certainly be replicated – they were just the wrong results.

To summarise, while it is certainly true that human behaviour is affected by numerous biases, we should remember that this also applies to scientists. Bear this in mind in the next chapter, where we look at how what might be called the 'rationality bias' shaped how economists dealt with – or rather, avoided dealing with – the role that basic human emotions play in the economy.

THE PLEASURE MACHINE 6

The neoclassical picture of human behaviour is summed up by independence and rationality. According to expected utility theory, a person makes decisions by computing which of the available options offers the maximum utility. And by utility, we mean that person's utility. As economist Francis Edgeworth wrote in his 1881 book *Mathematical Psychics*, 'The first principle of economics is that every agent is actuated only by self-interest.' A century later, prospect theory tweaked these assumptions by showing that our behaviour is more complex, but didn't fundamentally challenge them. In this picture, we are still trying to optimise utility, but sometimes we do a less-than-perfect job.

However, a corollary of these assumptions is that we don't let emotions interfere in the decision-making process, which doesn't seem very realistic. For one thing, if we are influenced by emotions such as fear or greed, then we probably won't make rational decisions. And if we feel empathy for others, then the focus on self-centred utility begins to look a little narrow.

There is also something inconsistent in the idea that emotion can be excluded from economics. The first neoclassical economists defined utility in terms of the pleasure that we gain from something, which is an emotional response. Edgeworth spoke about the 'Calculus of Pleasure', took it as an axiom that 'Pleasure is measurable, and all pleasures are commensurable', and wrote that '*the conception of Man as a pleasure machine* may justify and facilitate the employment of mechanical terms and Mathematical reasoning in social science' (emphasis in original).

Economists soon distanced themselves from this emphasis on pleasure, and began to speak in terms of preferences which were revealed through decisions and could be ranked in order. But in the 1970s, behavioural psychologists began to return to the idea of emotional states such as pleasure and pain. Kahneman and Tversky echoed Edgeworth a century later in their 1972 report when (in two places) they mentioned 'the nature of man as a pleasure machine'. They also added an evolutionary angle, explaining that our greater sensitivity to losses than to gains 'has adaptive value. Happy species endowed with infinite appreciation of pleasures and low sensitivity to pain would probably not survive the evolutionary battle.' The emphasis was on expected emotions – i.e. how much pleasure or pain one expected to derive from a decision – rather than the emotional states that are experienced at the actual time of decision. As Kahneman later said of their 1974 article, 'We documented systematic errors in the thinking of normal people, and we traced these errors to the design of the machinery of cognition rather than to the corruption of thought by emotion.' Emotion had therefore been reframed as just another mechanistic response.

We will return to the underlying assumption that 'Pleasure is measurable, and all pleasures are commensurable' in the final chapter. But for now, one of the differences between conscious people and machines is that machines don't feel pleasure. The reason we buy something is often exactly because it gives us a visceral feeling of pleasure or joy that defies exact quantification. As feminist economists have pointed out, the emphasis on rationality also has a gendered aspect (we return to this in the final chapter). And does everything in economics have to be related to some evolutionary battle for survival of the fittest? This chapter looks at the role of emotion in decision-making – and tries to answer the question, where did all the *feeling* go in economics?

How interesting

One way that emotion feeds into economic decision-making is through our attitude towards time. In his 1759 *Theory of Moral Sentiments*, Adam Smith noted that 'The pleasure which we are to enjoy ten years hence, interests us so little in comparison with that which we may enjoy to-day.' William Stanley Jevons, in his 1871 *Theory of Political Economy*, similarly observed that 'less commodity will be assigned to future days in some proportion to the intervening time', and addressed it mathematically by discounting future utility.

The first detailed theory of time preference, however, was developed by the US economist Irving Fisher in his 1930 book *The Theory of Interest*. He proposed that a person's level of impatience was decided by a combination of economic and personal factors. The first depended on the size and quality of the person's income: 'other things being equal, the smaller the income, the higher the preference for present over future income, that is the greater the impatience.' The personal factors he considered were foresight, self-control, habit, expectation of life, concern for the lives of other people, and fashion. Fisher stressed the irrational nature of things like a lack of self-control: 'Like those working men who, before prohibition, could not resist the lure of the saloon on the way home Saturday night, many persons cannot deny themselves a present indolence, even when they know what the consequences will be.' He described fashion, meanwhile, as 'one of those potent yet illusory forces which follow the laws of imitation'.

While Fisher acknowledged the role these personal factors played in decision making, he didn't allow them to affect his economic model, which like those of other neoclassical economists was based on the assumption that actors had perfect foresight, or what is now called rational expectations. Even if the level of impatience varied between people, one could always assume that the patient people lent money to the point where their impatience matched that of the people they were lending to. The interest rate charged would in theory approximate this aggregate level of impatience, plus the inflation rate.

Fisher summed this up in an equation which states that the nominal interest rate (the one that is usually reported) is equal to the real interest rate (which reflects the actual inflation-adjusted return that lenders demand) plus inflation. Inflation was harmful because of the 'money illusion' – i.e. our tendency to think in terms of nominal values rather than 'real' values – which made it hard to compare past costs with present costs (for example to understand whether selling your house for double what you paid was a great deal), or for businesses to raise prices without losing customers.

Fisher's method was based on graphics and was hard to extend for general situations. In 1937, a graduate student by the name of Paul Samuelson wrote a 'Note on the Measurement of Utility' which formalised and simplified Fisher's ideas into an elegant mathematical model, known as the discounted utility model, which could be applied for any time period. Samuelson went on to become one of the most influential economists of the twentieth century. And while Samuelson pointed out that people might have inconsistent time preferences, which would invalidate the theory, that did not stop his model from becoming the gold standard for describing time preferences in economics.

Of course, if a mathematical model can accurately discount utility into the distant future, then it followed that rational economic man could as well. A side effect of the theory was that economists began to apply their models over longer and longer time periods. An example was the question of a consumption function, which describes how we allocate a windfall payment: spend it or save it? In his *General Theory*, Keynes noted that the 'marginal propensity to consume' depends on the savings rate, which varies between social classes. If a family is granted £1,000, and the savings rate is 5 per cent, then they will spend £950 and save £50. In his 1957 *Theory of the Consumption Function*, Milton Friedman suggested a family would smooth their spending, so for example spend the £950 over three years rather than all at once. The same year, Franco Modigliani proposed that people smooth consumption over their entire lifetime, for example by borrowing when they are short of money and saving when they can. In this picture it therefore makes sense for students to borrow heavily to fund their university education.

It was only a matter of time before other economists such as Robert Barro were noting that rational economic man will propagate and have heirs, so his timescale is effectively infinite. This led to what economist J.W. Mason called in 2018 'the idea that the economy can be thought of as a single infinitely-lived individual calculating the trade-off between leisure and consumption over all future time. For an orthodox macroeconomist – anyone who hoped to be hired at a research university in the past thirty years – this approach isn't just one tool among others. It *is* macroeconomics.'

Discount plan

As Fisher pointed out, individual time preferences affect many economic decisions. A lack of self-control, for example, may tempt one into 'the saloon on the way home Saturday night' (which then was payday) but more generally it plays a role in the outcome of any decision which requires action on our part. And just as cognitive heuristics act as a kind of shortcut which saves mental energy, so self-control involves active work that we may tend to avoid. This is a problem because many of the most important economic decisions – such as investing for retirement, choosing a career, and so on – have outcomes that rely not just on the rational calculation of utility, but also on our ability to follow through with those decisions.

This was famously illustrated by a series of experiments in the 1960s and 1970s, led by psychologist Walter Mischel, in which nursery-age children were offered the choice between one treat (a marshmallow or cookie) immediately, or two if they could wait for a quarter hour while left alone in an empty room. The children employed various diversionary tactics, such as turning around so they couldn't see the tray. Some apparently would 'stroke the marshmallow as if it were a tiny stuffed animal'.

Those children who succeeded in waiting (about a third of the participants) were found, according to a 1990 follow-up paper, to have done better on a range of measures including SAT scores and educational attainment. An attempt to replicate the experiment in 2018 showed that the situation was more complicated, because the ability to delay gratification (and perhaps even trust that a second treat will be forthcoming) was itself linked to socio-economic factors. People from a rougher background may have learned earlier the adage that 'a bird in the hand is worth two in the bush'.

A deeper problem for economic models than the issue of self-control, though, is that time preferences aren't fixed, but themselves change with time. According to standard theory, time preference can be expressed using a discount factor which reflects our degree of patience or impatience. Just as financial markets discount future gains or losses according to the prevailing interest rate, so we discount future utility by some amount which depends on our own personal discount rate.

This discount rate is widely used in economics, often with rather perverse results. For example, the cost of future climate change depends on what discount rate you apply to the utility of having a functioning climate system. Set the discount rate low enough, and preventative action can be made to look too expensive. Similar arguments can be applied to justify procrastination on dealing with future needs of anything from healthcare to social security.

Going hyperbolic

Even at an individual level, though, the notion that we make decisions based on a fixed discount rate doesn't hold up. If the model were true, then it should apply equally across time periods. Suppose that a person is willing to pay £1 for a chocolate if they can have it now, but only £0.90 if they have to wait until tomorrow. For the equation to be consistent, this suggests a discount rate of 10 per cent per day. If we then asked how much the same person would pay for a chocolate if they have to wait one year, then we would have to apply that discount rate successively 365 times, which would value the chocolate treat at an amount indistinguishable from zero.

So imagine that we asked the same person how much they would value a far superior chocolate concoction which will still be worth £1 in one year's time. And then ask how much they would be willing to pay if its availability were to be delayed by an extra day, so 366 days instead of 365. For consistency, that extra day should again lower the value to £0.90.

Obviously neither of these features is realistic. Behavioural economists therefore came up with a scheme known as hyperbolic discounting, which adjusts the discount rate as a function of time in such a way as to privilege short time periods. This reflects the behavioural bias known as present bias, which makes a sharp distinction between *right now* and any delay. One reason why at least some stores selling physical books have managed to survive the Amazon era is that customers like to get their hands on a title immediately, even if it may cost considerably more than ordering online and waiting a few days. Another option is overnight delivery – apparently those who are willing to pay more for this service score lowly on something called the Cognitive Reflection Test, which tests how impulsive their decision-making is.

It seems that a constant feature of our economic lives is a battle between present bias and self-control – taking the marshmallow now or choosing to wait. One way to interpret this is through two-system models, such as Kahneman and Tversky's fast System 1 versus slow System 2. Thaler proposed a planner–doer model along similar lines, with the planner attempting to make rational decisions and the doer focusing more on the present moment. Though neither model was explicitly based on biology, Thaler pictured the planner as relying on the prefrontal cortex, and the doer on the limbic system.

Many businesses selling diet plans, or aids to stop smoking, have been set up to help with this mental conflict. Today, as mentioned in Chapter 3, many of these firms use techniques from behavioural psychology to help us meet our goals. However, people also adopt their own strategies. One method that people use to save money is mental accounting: the marginal propensity to save money is much higher if the source of the funds is a retirement savings account than if it is from a lottery win, which makes sense because people treat the money differently. Another is pre-commitment: by publicly committing to a goal, a person is more likely to see it through. This doesn't always work, as proved by the many gym memberships which go renewed but unused. And sometimes we don't get the balance right – for example when people have plenty of accumulated wealth in the forms of a house or a pension plan, but won't use it to pay off a lot of expensive credit card debt. A kind of inverse present bias occurs, meanwhile, when the emotion known as 'dread' impels us to get something that we know will be unpleasant over with as quickly as possible.

Present bias, of course, applies not just to humans, but to animals as well. A 1974 paper called 'Impulse Control In Pigeons' by George Ainslie related a version of the marshmallow experiment, in which it was found that pigeons had even less self-discipline than nursery children: 'Pigeons were given a small, immediate food reinforcement for pecking a key, and a larger, delayed reinforcement for not pecking this key. Most subjects pecked the key on more than 95% of trials.' On the other hand, we have grey squirrels, who hoard nuts for the winter but then often can't find them.

Smile!

While present bias makes us put more emphasis on what is happening right now, another kind of bias distorts the way we see the future. It is known as the optimism bias, and it appears to particularly afflict professional forecasters, whose job it is to look into the future.

A good example of the overly sunny nature of economic forecasts was the financial crisis of 2007–8. Not only did few economists predict it, they were also too positive about the recovery, which proved rather slower than expected. In April 2007, for example, the IMF said that: 'Notwithstanding the recent bout of financial volatility, the world economy still looks well set for continued robust growth in 2007 and 2008.' A year later, they were predicting a 'mild recession' in the US to be followed by a 'modest recovery' in 2009. Instead, US gross domestic product shrank by 3.5 per cent in 2009.

The IMF is far from unique – other organisations such

as the OECD failed to spot the dangers, as did surveys of individual economists. Part of the reason is that optimism is always popular, especially in areas such as business, because it makes everyone feel good. As Kahneman wrote in *Thinking, Fast and Slow*, 'Most of us view the world as more benign than it really is, our own attributes as more favorable than they truly are, and the goals we adopt as more achievable than they are likely to be.'

An exception, as discussed in the first chapter, was the Bank of England's forecast for the short-term impact of Brexit, which proved far too pessimistic. Indeed, as Kahneman notes, if we are usually too optimistic about the future, we are even more optimistic about our powers of prediction: 'We also tend to exaggerate our ability to forecast the future, which fosters overconfidence.' This confidence is particularly valued in times of crisis, since 'Extreme uncertainty is paralyzing under dangerous circumstances, and the admission that one is merely guessing is especially unacceptable when the stakes are high'. Because of its role in decision-making, 'the optimistic bias may well be the most significant of the cognitive biases'.

As forecasting experts Spyros Makridakis and Nassim Taleb agreed in an article in the *International Journal of Forecasting*, 'Empirical evidence has shown that the ability of people to correctly assess uncertainty is even worse than that of accurately predicting future outcomes. Such evidence has shown that humans are overconfident of positive expectations, while ignoring or downgrading negative information.' Forecasters, it seems, are mirroring a basic human trait in their optimistic stance – which is a problem if they do not pick up signals warning of impending disasters, or fail to take into account the full range of possibilities.

Superforecasters

One way to compensate for the cognitive biases that affect forecasting is the method known as 'reference class forecasting', which was developed in the 1970s by Kahneman and Tversky. Given a particular project – such as the building of a new transportation system – the steps are to identify a group of similar projects; establish a probability distribution for whatever is being predicted, such as usage; and finally compare the new project with the others. However, this approach relies on the existence of comparable projects.

Instead of asking experts directly, an alternative is to use prediction markets that allow people to bet on outcomes of events such as elections. These were inspired by economic theories such as the efficient market theory, which as discussed later view markets as unbeatable prediction machines. For example, the price of a contract that pays $1 in the event of a particular election result should converge on the expected value (so if there is a 40 per cent probability, the contract should be worth $0.40).

While prediction markets have a relatively good track record, it seems they can be beaten by teams made up of what political scientist Philip Tetlock calls 'superforecasters': individuals who have demonstrated a consistent ability to make good forecasts. Prediction competitions, which set specific questions such as 'will event A happen in the next six months?', found that teams of forecasters beat the 'wisdom of the crowd' (e.g., a general poll) by 10 per cent; prediction markets beat those teams by about 20 per cent; while teams composed of superforecasters beat prediction markets by 15 to 30 per cent.

An example was the 2014 Scottish referendum on leaving the United Kingdom, in which 'no' won by a large margin of 55.3 per cent to 44.7 per cent, even though late polls showed a dead heat. 'Superforecasters aced this one,' wrote Tetlock, 'even beating British betting markets with real money on the table.' However, they did less well on Brexit, giving only a 23 per cent chance of Britain leaving the European Union. (Of course, these are both probabilistic predictions so perfect accuracy is not expected.)

So what is a superforecaster? According to Tetlock, 'They score higher than average on measures of intelligence and open-mindedness, although they are not off the charts. What makes them so good is less what they are than what they do – the hard work of research, the careful thought and self-criticism, the gathering and synthesizing of other perspectives, the granular judgements and relentless updating.'

Denial

Closely connected with optimism bias is its chief enabler, denial.

One of the greatest talents of the human race is our capacity for denial. Without the ability to deny reality, it would be hard to get through the day. We would have to face up to all sorts of scary and unwelcome facts, such as death, the ballooning national debt, climate change, the heat death of the universe, numerous personal failings, and so on.

A believer in human rationality might argue that, while we may make many decisions using what Kahneman and Tversky called System 1 thinking, which is prone to avoiding unpleasant realities, we always have left-brained System 2 to act as a corrective backup. As Kahneman points out, though, the reality is somewhat different. We make decisions quickly, and then rationalise them so they make sense. When it comes to things like personal attitudes, 'System 2 is more of an apologist for the emotions of System 1 than a critic of those emotions – an endorser rather than an enforcer'.

According to Kahneman, 'The sense-making machinery of System 1 makes us see the world as more tidy, simple, predictable, and coherent than it really is. The illusion that one has understood the past feeds the further illusion that one can predict and control the future. These illusions are comforting. They reduce the anxiety that we would experience if we allowed ourselves to fully acknowledge the uncertainties of existence.' System 2 doesn't want to spoil the party.

Again, a good example of this can be seen in the field of economic forecasting. As we'll see later, the key idea behind economics and finance prior to the 2007–8 crisis was that markets are naturally driven to a state of stable equilibrium. Markets are therefore 'efficient' in the sense that everything is priced correctly. In the eyes of most people, the financial crisis didn't seem to back up the notion that markets are efficient and self-equilibrating. Yet economists seemed to be in denial. Questioned about the theory in 2010, Eugene Fama (winner of the 2013 economics Nobel) said, 'I think it did quite well in this episode.' Tom Sargent (winner of the 2011 economics Nobel) said in 2011 that 'It is just wrong to say that this financial crisis caught modern macroeconomists by surprise.' Robert Lucas (1995 economics Nobel) admitted the crisis had not been predicted but saw this as a natural result of Fama's efficient market hypothesis. In fact, many economists confabulated the crisis into a kind of validation of their theories – including, apparently, those on the Nobel committee.

Let's talk about sex

While time preferences and cognitive biases certainly play an important role in economics, things get much more complicated when we consider that many economic decisions are influenced not just by cognitive judgements or sunny optimism but by raw emotions and passions.

As an example of the kind of thing we're talking about, consider the 2006 paper 'The Heat of the Moment: The Effect of Sexual Arousal on Sexual Decision Making' by behavioural psychologists Dan Ariely and George Loewenstein. I will let the abstract speak for itself:

> Despite the social importance of decisions taken in the 'heat of the moment', very little research has examined the effect of sexual arousal on judgment and decision making. Here we examine the effect of sexual arousal, induced by self-stimulation, on judgments and hypothetical decisions made by male college students. Students were assigned to be in either a state of sexual arousal or a neutral state and were asked to: (1) indicate how appealing they find a wide range of sexual stimuli and activities, (2) report their willingness to engage in morally questionable behavior in order to obtain sexual gratification, and (3) describe their willingness to engage in unsafe sex when sexually aroused. The results show that sexual arousal had a strong impact on all three areas of judgment and decision making, demonstrating the importance of situational forces on

preferences, as well as subjects' inability to predict these influences on their own behavior.

This is exactly the kind of test that you couldn't do, even as a thought experiment, using rational economic man. The results unsurprisingly showed that male college students behave in a manner which is more risk-friendly when aroused than when taking a metaphorical cold shower: 'the increase in motivation to have sex produced by sexual arousal seems to decrease the relative importance of other considerations such as behaving ethically toward a potential sexual partner or protecting oneself against unwanted pregnancy or sexually transmitted disease.' The reason is that 'sexual arousal seems to narrow the focus of motivation, creating a kind of tunnel-vision where goals other than sexual fulfilment become eclipsed by the motivation to have sex'. At the same time, 'people seem to have only limited insight into the impact of sexual arousal on their own judgments and behavior.' Ariely concluded from such experiments that 'Our models of human behavior need to be rethought. Perhaps there is no such thing as a fully integrated human being. We may, in fact, be an agglomeration of multiple selves.'

This might seem unrelated to economics, until you consider that pornography, according to the *New York Times*, 'is one of the most consumed forms of media in the world. Pornhub, the popular pornography website, draws 80 million visitors a day. Exact figures for the size of the industry are scarce, but experts put total sales around a billion dollars a year.' Yet the industry comes under remarkably little scrutiny for things like piracy, working conditions, or ethical violations. As Shira Tarrant, author of *The Pornography Industry*, said in an interview, one reason is that 'People are getting sexually aroused and they just kind of go into a political or economic denial about what they're doing. And then also, we live in a culture that doesn't want to talk about sex or sexuality.' Nowhere is that more true than in mainstream economics, where for all the talk of pleasure and pain, there has been remarkably little room for real human drives and emotions.

Moving out

More generally, visceral emotions play an important role every time we decide to engage in an economic transaction. The word 'emotion' comes from Latin roots meaning 'out' (*ex*) and 'move' (*movere*). Reason can tell us what we *should* do, but emotion impels us to actually do it (or something else). Prospect theory is based on abstract prospects or gambles where people are asked to choose between different games. In real life, people gamble because they think it is fun. When most people visit a casino or buy a ticket in a lottery, they aren't setting out to rationally optimise their utility, they are enjoying the sense of possibility. Stock market returns have been shown to correlate with the weather, presumably because good weather imbues traders with a sunny sense of optimism. We refrain from exorbitant spending not just in order to optimise future utility, but because wasting money makes us feel bad. Business negotiations rely on emotions, and can fall apart quickly if one party becomes angry, or embarrassed.

And of course we do things, such as voluntary work, because helping others can make us feel happy. This behaviour is not limited to humans: one experiment found, for example, that African grey parrots help birds in adjacent cages get food despite there being no benefit to themselves.

Indeed, as George Loewenstein pointed out in a 2000 paper, 'it is probably not an overstatement to say that visceral factors are more basic to daily functioning than the higher-level cognitive processes that are often assumed to underlie decision-making.' He notes that, while the capacity for abstract reasoning might not be widely shared with animals (see pigeons, squirrels), we do share the same capacity for 'emotions and other visceral factors'. Yet these other animals seem to get through their lives quite adequately. A bee colony, for example, seems pretty organised and efficient.

According to Loewenstein, while visceral factors such as emotion have 'traditionally been seen as an erratic and unpredictable influence on behavior', this 'changeability should not be confused … with unpredictability'. He gives the example of a cocaine addict, who goes through repeated cycles of binge and withdrawal while engaging in 'elaborate self-control strategies and self-deception'. When rats are given access to an unlimited supply of cocaine, in contrast, they just take it until they collapse or die. Dan Ariely also showed that people tend to make choices from a selection of products more consistently when they are emotionally engaged with the products. In fact, studies of patients who for neurological reasons are unable to process emotional information show that it is extremely hard to make decisions without some emotional input.

Loewenstein therefore proposed that visceral factors could be modelled as motivational factors, which act like a carrot and a stick. We are motivated to eat because we feel hungry, and this in turn heightens our enjoyment of the food. Anger acts as a stick which brings out aggression. The utility function u should therefore be a function not just of consumption, but also of the person's visceral state.

Emotions also affect the way we make decisions under risk, because our emotional response to risk is not the same as our cognitive response: we may fear things that do not seem risky, or not fear things that strike us objectively as dangerous. The reason is that 'the determinants of fear are different from the determinants of cognitive evaluations of riskiness'. For example, many people are viscerally afraid of snakes, but not so afraid of fast-moving cars, which are far more dangerous. Fear of an upcoming event may grow as the moment approaches, leading to the phenomenon known as 'chickening out'. And it will not come as news to marketers that emotions play a key role in purchase decisions, or that our sense of risk is balanced by a sense of fun and excitement, or that these effects can be manipulated – as with cigarette advertising, in places where it has not been banned.

According to Loewenstein, one reason economists traditionally left visceral factors out of their analysis might be 'because they are seen as too unpredictable and complex to be amenable to formal modeling'. While he argues that emotions are in fact quite predictable, incorporating emotions and other visceral effects would complicate economics in two ways. One is that emotions such as anger often make people act in a way which is not in their own best interest (e.g. road rage), which undercuts rather the whole idea of utility maximisation. Another is that people consistently misjudge the effect of such emotions, which again leads to sub-optimal behaviour – for example, deciding to experiment with drugs that are known to be highly addictive. It turns out that the best way to avoid temptation – in anything from sex to drugs – is not to exert iron-like self-control, but just to avoid situations where one is likely to be tempted in the first place. If you have a gambling problem, avoid casinos.

Scanner

The role of emotions has been further explored and elucidated by researchers working in neuroeconomics, the marriage of behavioural economics and neuroscience which first emerged around the start of the millennium. Instead of just asking experimental subjects questions like normal behavioural economists, neuroeconomists first put their subjects in scanners, and then ask them questions. By monitoring which areas of the brain light up (i.e. are drawing the most blood, which correlates with neuron firing), they can tell how the person is processing the information and formulating their response – and whether they are acting on logic or emotion.

For example, scans have shown that the offer of a reward affects different parts of the brain depending on whether the reward is immediate or delayed. The former triggers a stronger response, consistent with present bias. When patient people think about the future, they use the brain region that is usually active when they think about themselves; but when impatient people think about the future, that region is quiet, as if they see their future self as somebody different. Similarly, when we think about death, we think about it as something that happens to other people.

In general, it seems that most of our automatic, System 1 thinking takes place in the limbic system, particularly the structure known as the amygdala, which is located in the middle area of the brain. Logical, controlled, System 2 thinking takes place in the front or prefrontal cortex, which is sometimes known as the 'executive region' because it integrates inputs from other parts of the brain and draws up long-term plans.

As the Harvard economist David Laibson told the *New Yorker* in 2006: 'Natural science has moved ahead by studying progressively smaller units. Physicists started out studying the stars, then they looked at objects, molecules, atoms, subatomic particles, and so on. My sense is that economics is going to follow the same path. Forty years ago, it was mainly about large-scale phenomena, like inflation and unemployment. More recently, there has been a lot of focus on individual decision-making. I think the time has now come to go beyond the individual and look at the inputs to individual decision-making. That is what we do in neuroeconomics.'

The embodied mind

Of course, the idea that we can interpret human emotions as fluxes in brain activity will sound to many like the ultimate example of reductionist social science – as if we have finally worked out a way to take the human 'pleasure machine' apart into pieces. An alternative view of the mind/body connection is taken by a number of feminist thinkers, who point out that since the time of the ancient Greeks, Western philosophy has been based on a dualistic view which places the rational mind in opposition with the 'base' properties of the body. The former has traditionally been characterised as male, the latter as female. As science writer Margaret Wertheim notes, mathematics in particular was 'an inherently masculine task. Mathematics was associated with the gods, and with transcendence from the material world; women, by their nature, were supposedly rooted in this latter, baser realm.'

This traditional dualistic view, which survives in modified form in behavioural economics, is challenged by the theory of embodied cognition, which argues that many aspects of cognition are shaped not just in the brain through computation, but by the entire body. As an example, a 2014 study by psychologists Eun Hee Lee and Simone Schnall tested whether 'social power affects the perception of physical properties of objects' by making their subjects lift heavy boxes. They found that people who felt themselves to be socially powerful experienced the box as being less heavy. Other experiments showed that the experience of a steep uphill climb was eased if the subject did it with a friend, or were in a good mood, or had a glucose boost.

Indeed, it seems that emotional, cognitive, and physical effort all draw, at least to a degree, on a common reserve of mental energy. The nervous system in general, and mental effort in particular, is one of the body's leading users of glucose. This was graphically illustrated in a study of eight parole judges in Israel, which showed that their judgements varied depending on whether they had recently had a meal break, with the chances of granting parole declining to nearly zero just before the next feeding time.

The mind can also be affected by the body in other ways. In one experiment, people listened to talks through headphones and were asked to move their heads repeatedly, in order (they were told) to check the reliability of the equipment. One group was told to nod their head up and down, the other to shake it left and right. When asked about the message of the talk, the first group was more likely to agree with it.

Such studies show that cognition cannot be viewed in isolation from the body. More generally, as the psychologist Iain McGilchrist notes, the brain should be seen not as 'a cognitive machine, a computer that is fitted with a *rule-based programme* for structuring the world' (his emphasis), but rather as 'an embodied, living organism'.

While behavioural economists often speak of the brain as having two systems, it is curious that this ignores the most obvious feature of the brain, which is that it is divided neatly into two hemispheres with different but complementary specialities. According to McGilchrist, the sense of embodiment, like related functions including emotional expressivity, is rooted in the brain's right hemisphere. (An exception is anger, which is a left hemisphere speciality.) The left hemisphere, meanwhile, prefers 'what is mechanical' and its 'principal concern is utility'. The left brain is computational, the right brain is not.

The insistence in the social sciences on treating the human brain as a cognitive machine is perhaps why the brain's 'deeply divided structure has remained largely unexplained and even unexamined' by psychologists (with some exceptions). It is as if our divided brains have shielded us from studying those very divisions. Economics – including the development of prospect theory – begins to seem like another example of the phenomenon, described in McGilchrist's book *The Master and his Emissary*, of the left hemisphere repressing the role of the right hemisphere, and trying to usurp its function.

The specialised role of brain hemispheres applies not just to humans, but to birds and animals. The left hemisphere 'yields narrow, focussed attention, mainly for the purpose of getting and feeding. The right hemisphere yields a broad, vigilant attention, the purpose of which appears to be awareness of signals from the surroundings, especially of other creatures, who are potential predators or potential mates, foes or friends; and it is involved in bonding in social animals.' As we will see in the next chapter, nowhere is the tension between these mental forces more evident than in the social institution known as markets.

SAFETY IN NUMBERS 7

As mentioned in Chapter 2, neoclassical economics was explicitly based on Newtonian mechanics. The idea was to reduce the system to parts, analyse the forces that acted on the parts, express them using mathematical equations, and solve. The result was a mathematical model of the system. In economics, the atoms of the system were rational individuals who took decisions in isolation and acted to optimise their own utility. This chapter shows how this atomistic, mechanistic model is used in the world of finance – and how behavioural economics challenges it.

In 1921 Keynes criticised what he called the 'atomic character of natural law. The system of the material universe,' he wrote, 'must consist, if this kind of assumption is warranted, of bodies which we may term legal atoms, such that each of them exercises its own separate, independent, and invariable effect.' Rather than abandon it, however, post-war era economists took the physics analogy in two different directions. On the one hand, they doubled down on independence and rationality, to produce results such as the Arrow–Debreu 'invisible hand' theorem, which granted economic 'atoms' the ability to look into the future.

At the same time, though, a new breed of economist, inspired by ideas from quantum physics, argued that markets were subject to random forces that made them essentially unpredictable. These developments led to one of the most influential theories in the history of economics, known as the efficient market hypothesis, which was a kind of economic version of the uncertainty principle from physics.

The random walk

In a 1965 paper titled 'Random walks in stock-market prices', based on his PhD thesis, Eugene Fama described an efficient market as a place in which 'competition among the many intelligent participants' leads to a situation where the price of a security accurately reflects all available information, and therefore corresponds to the security's 'intrinsic value' as reflected by its potential for future earnings.

In such a market, price changes were driven solely by the arrival of new information. Because that information is random, the price of a stock or other asset can be modelled using what mathematicians call a random walk. The price takes a step up or down, and gradually tends to get further from its starting point. However, it is impossible to predict its next move, or where it will be in a day, a month, or a year. Stock pickers or market analysts who claim they can look into the future are deluding themselves and/or their customers.

In some ways, the efficient market hypothesis seemed to back up the idea that markets are driven to a stable equilibrium. According to Fama, 'Tests of market efficiency are tests of some model of market equilibrium and vice versa. The two are joined at the hip.' Or as Thaler later put it, 'To simplify somewhat, we can say that Optimization + Equilibrium = Economics. This is a powerful combination, nothing that other social sciences can match.' On the other hand, it led to a weird situation where rational economic man is assumed to be able to make perfect predictions, but this in turn means that no one can predict the markets.

The idea that highly rational traders drive prices to their perfect level obviously seems incompatible, to say the least, with our observed cognitive shortcomings. In *Phishing for Phools*, Akerlof and Shiller compare the behaviour of investors to Capuchin monkeys, who can be trained to use money to bargain in markets. The monkeys also have a weakness for treats such as Marshmallow Fluff-filled Fruit Roll-Ups – but if they eat too many they become 'anxious, malnourished, exhausted, addicted, quarrelsome, and sickened'. In other words, they behave exactly like human traders. According to the authors, competitive pressures in the market may drive the economy to a state of equilibrium, but part of that process is clever 'phishers' taking advantage of vulnerable 'phools' by exploiting their cognitive weaknesses and lack of information.

Behavioural economics has taught us a lot about our monkey-like cognitive traits – but what does it have to say about these core notions of market equilibrium and efficiency? And does it offer a real challenge to mainstream ideas like the efficient market hypothesis?

People do a lot of nutty things

If equilibrium theory and efficient market theory are joined at the hip, then one of the assumptions which bandages them together – and which forms the basis for theories of finance – is the idea that people are rational and independent. As seen in earlier chapters, the rationality assumption doesn't hold up very well; however, in itself this might not be such a big problem for mainstream theory, because it can always be argued that these effects wash out on average, or have little effect on their own, or go away as we learn. As economist John Cochrane puts it: 'People do a lot of nutty things. But when you raise the price of tomatoes, they buy fewer tomatoes, just as if utility maximizers had walked into the grocery store.'

As Akerlof and Shiller note, this tendency to downplay behavioural effects has been reinforced by the tendency of behavioural economists themselves to treat deviations from rationality on a 'case-by-case basis – but just as rare exceptions. This message is not intended, but the presentation of behavioral economics, perhaps unconsciously, yields this implication.' This scattershot approach also means that few results have real statistical power, of the sort that can be aggregated up to make robust predictions about the economy as a whole. (As Fama put it during a debate with Thaler, 'There's a difference between anecdotes and evidence, right?') And even if some people do make mistakes, like pay too much for a stock, or sell too cheaply, then the 'smart money' will take advantage of them and drive prices back to their correct level. As Chicago economist Gary Becker put it, division of labour 'strongly attenuates if not eliminates any effects' caused by lapses in rationality, as 'it doesn't matter if 90 percent of people can't do the complex analysis required to calculate probabilities. The 10 percent of people who can will end up in the jobs where it's required.'

The concept of rationality is also remarkably malleable, which makes its absence hard to prove. For example, if a person – or for that matter a Fruit Roll-Up-loving monkey – appears to be sacrificing future utility for short-term gain, then an economist can just redefine the individual's utility function so that it is weighted for short-term gain, and presto, they are now acting rationally. Evolutionary biology can be evoked to say that apparently irrational behaviour can bestow some long-term genetic advantage which is selected for because it supplies 'an edge in the mating game', as one economist put it. Phenomena such as booms and crashes which seem to be driven by outbursts of collective madness can be reinterpreted as rational, especially if you take predictability as your criterion. As Fama stated in 2016: 'I don't think there is any concrete evidence of bubbles. A bubble to me means something that has a predictable ending. But nobody has ever been able to identify any predictability in financial markets.'

And anomalies can always be addressed by adding more bells and whistles to the model. For example, some economists have argued that small companies outperform large ones, and companies that have done well recently will continue in the near term to outperform those that haven't. According to efficient market theory, they shouldn't, because that would imply that small firms for example are undervalued. One way out, though, is to say that smaller firms are riskier, and the cheaper valuation therefore reflects a 'risk premium' which can be added to the model. The only problem with this argument is that standard measures of risk don't show that smaller firms are riskier, but again, that can be debated forever.

Many therefore believe that behavioural quirks mostly wash out at larger scales. Or as law professor William

Hubbard put it in a 2017 paper, 'In the realm of physics, the Correspondence Principle tells us that Newtonian mechanics is basically wrong, but it's a pretty good approximation at the scale of human society, most but not all of the time. The analogous principle in behavioral economics is that neoclassical economics is basically wrong, but it's a pretty good approximation at the scale of human society, most but not all of the time.'

Indeed, the reality is that behavioural economists usually refrain from challenging the broader conclusions of neoclassical economics. In a 1985 talk, Robert Shiller rejected the idea of a revolution 'leading to the abandonment of assumptions of rational expectations'. Instead he saw behavioural models as extensions that would lead to 'the enhancement of the efficient market models', and could teach the latter 'with much more relish if I could describe them as extreme special cases before moving to the more realistic models'. In *Thinking, Fast and Slow*, Kahneman similarly wrote that raising questions about basic concepts would be 'confusing, and perhaps demoralizing' for students. 'Furthermore, the failure of rationality that is built into prospect theory is often irrelevant to the predictions of economic theory, which work out with great precision in some situations and provide good approximations in many others.' Only in some contexts does 'the difference become significant'. Nor does behavioural economics really question the idea that people should behave rationally – only that we aren't as good at it as economists usually assumed in their models. Viewed this way, the above-noted tendency of behavioural economists to focus on 'rare exceptions' to the neoclassical model looks like a rather successful strategy to win mainstream acceptance – a feature rather than a bug.

As we'll see below, though, behavioural economics is potentially destabilising for mainstream theory in at least one way – and it is not about rationality so much as the properties of networks, communication, and human connection.

Ultimatum

Mainstream economics is based, as we have seen, on the idea of rational economic man, who is assumed to be both rational and independent. As the seventeenth-century English poet John Donne pointed out, though (perhaps while reflecting on Brexit): 'No man is an Island, entire of itself; every man is a piece of the Continent, a part of the main.' Even a rational economic one. This principle has been exhaustively tested by behavioural psychologists who have proved that not only are we not islands, but our behaviour is strongly influenced by the social groups in which we are embedded.

One reason is that in social systems such as the economy, everything is relative. We only know how much something is worth by comparing it with the prices of other things. And while utility theory assumes that we act to maximise our own utility, that doesn't take into account the fact that part of that utility is our position relative to others. A financial transaction isn't just a question of money, it is also about relations between people.

This was famously illustrated in an experiment known as the ultimatum game. A prize of, say, £10 is to be divided between two people. The wrinkle is that one person gets to decide how the award will be split. If the other person rejects the offer, then the prize is lost.

According to classical theory, the second player should accept any offer greater than zero, since that will optimise their utility. In practice – and the experiment has been repeated many times in different countries – most offers are close to an equal split, and offers below £2 or £3 tend to be rejected, just because they are annoying. From the standpoint of maximising expected profit, rather than fairness, the best offer turns out to be around £4, since lower offers also carry a higher risk of being rejected.

By carrying out the game while people are in scanners, neuroscientists have showed that the part of the brain involved in the rejection of unfair offers is the bilateral anterior insula, which is associated with anger and disgust. As with the prisoner's dilemma (see page 28), what counts is not just individual utility but social context. The same sense of fair play is shared with animals: in tests where dogs or wolves were rewarded for performing tasks, 'if one animal was given a more substantial reward when performing a task, the other one downed tools completely.'

Comedy of the commons

Concepts such as efficiency and optimality therefore become much more complicated when feelings are involved. And social behaviour is affected not just by our emotional connection with other people, but also by social norms. This is illustrated in our approach to what economists call public goods. In economics, a public good is a resource that can be used by anyone, and is non-rivalrous in the sense that its use by one person doesn't reduce its use by another. An example would be a flood control system, or a lighthouse, or a fireworks display. A common good is similar except that it may be rivalrous, so can potentially be dominated by a small group.

Either of these goods fit uneasily with the neoclassical viewpoint. The idea of a public good was first defined by Paul Samuelson in a 1954 paper, in which he argued that public goods will be undersupplied in a free-market economy because even if they are beneficial, people won't pay for them.

Similarly, in his 1968 paper 'The Tragedy of the Commons', the ecologist Garrett Hardin described a kind of parable, in which a number of animal herders all have access to an area of common pasture. For each herder, rational self-interest dictates that they should exploit as much of the land as possible; but if they all do this, then the result is over-grazing, so no one benefits.

The conclusion in either case appears to be that resources need to be managed either privately or by the state. As the political scientist Elinor Ostrom argued, however, a variety of commons around the world – including forestries, fisheries, irrigation systems, grasslands, and so on – are being sustainably managed, in defiance of economic principles (Ostrom was awarded the economics Nobel for her work, the first of only two to go to a woman so far). Behavioural economists have also explored the same ground through the use of experiments with what is known as the public good game.

In the basic version of this game, a number of people are given some tokens, and are asked to put however many they choose into a public pot. The tokens in the pot are multiplied by a factor which is greater than one. The pot is then divided equally between the players.

As an example, suppose there are 40 players, and each starts with tokens worth 2. If each player contributes 1 to the pot, then the pot will be worth 40. If the pot were then divided equally, everyone would just get their token back. But let's say that the pot is multiplied by a factor 1.3, which reflects the synergy that emerges when everyone contributes to a common cause. The pot will then be worth 52, so after it is divided each player gets 1.3, on top of the 1 they kept, for a total 2.3. If instead each person had contributed 2, and held nothing back, then the pot of 80 would grow to 104, and after division each player would end up with 2.6, which is the maximum possible.

According to the dictates of classical game theory, the correct move for rational economic man is to donate 0. In the worst case he keeps his 2 tokens. In the best case, everyone except for him donates the full amount, and he makes out like a bandit (the so-called free rider problem).

In practice, however, few people take this approach. For the version described above, with 40 participants and a multiplication factor of 1.3, the average contribution is about half of the initial endowment. Again, the reason is that people have social norms for things like generosity and community-mindedness. Indeed, in some versions of the game participants will even pay to punish free riders – just as they are happy in the ultimatum game to reject an overly cheap offer. As the economist Amaryta Sen put it, 'The purely economic man is indeed close to being a social moron. Economic theory has been much preoccupied with this rational fool.'

In a 1993 paper that Thaler later described as 'the most important theory paper in behavioral economics since "Prospect Theory"', the behavioural economist Matthew Rabin proposed that the reason for this apparently irrational behaviour 'hinges on reciprocity. We are nice to people who treat us nicely and mean to people who treat us badly.'

Interestingly, while the experiment has been repeated among different groups and contexts, there is one group of people who seem particularly prone to the free-rider problem, which is economists. As the sociologists Gerald Marwell and Ruth Ames discovered, an education in economics has the effect of dropping the contribution rate from 50 per cent to 20 per cent – not that surprising given that they have been trained to see the world through the eyes of rational economic man.

Identity economics

As seen in earlier chapters, one reason we have cognitive biases is because making decisions is hard, so we take shortcuts. And when we make judgements about different prospects, we do so by comparing them to a reference point. But the biggest shortcut of all is just to copy what other people are doing – and the most important reference point is our peers.

This was illustrated in a 2000 paper by George Akerlof and Rachel Kranton titled 'Economics and Identity'. As Kranton told *World Finance* in an interview, 'The way we define who we are, the way we define who others are, the way that impacts how we make decisions, was not present' in existing economic models. Their approach was to modify the utility function in such a way that it took the person's identity into account. The utility of an action depends on the action itself, but also on whether it is consistent with the person's sense of identity, which can add or subtract utility. Since identity is in part constructed through affiliation with social groups, it followed that preferences were to some extent socially constructed. And because social norms change over time, a person's preferences do as well.

An example is gender politics, where social norms have shifted dramatically in the last few decades. As Kranton notes, 'It's not that the brains and the bodies of women have changed. It's how we understand gender.'

It also turns out that our alignment with social groups can be surprisingly fickle. This was demonstrated in a series of experiments by psychologist Muzafer Sherif. In a 1954 experiment, he and his colleagues invited 22 eleven-year-old boys to attend a remote summer camp in Robbers Cave State Park, Oklahoma. The boys were divided into two groups and assigned to separate cabins, far enough away that they didn't know of the other group's existence. During the first week, each group chose a name – The Eagles, and The Rattlers – and bonded through shared activities such as hiking and swimming.

In the second week, the groups were brought into contact. The researchers, who were disguised as camp counsellors, set up competitions between them. Soon the groups were in open conflict, to the point where they were raiding each other's cabins, burning the other side's flags, and so on. After four days, the researchers initiated a two-day cooling-off period, where the boys were asked to assess their own group (very favourable) and the other group (very bad).

As a more sedate example, I experienced this group identity effect while participating in a scenario-planning workshop at RAND in 2012. A group of transport and forecasting experts had been tasked by the US Department of Transport to describe what the US transport system might look like in 40 years' time. In order to generate ideas, we divided into four different groups, with the titles Business As Usual, Tech

Triumphs, Gentle Footprint, and (my group) Global Chaos. As the names suggest, each group was to take a different position – that things would continue in much the same fashion as today, that we would live in a high-technology utopia, that environmentalists would take over, or that the world would go to hell and countries would retreat into isolation.

The way it worked was that we would each make a pitch for why our scenario was the most realistic, and then criticise the other scenarios. Even though we were assigned to groups at random, it soon became clear that we were all identifying quite strongly with our respective positions. For my part, I found myself making what seemed to me like utterly convincing arguments for the inevitability of the coming apocalypse. And I'm sticking to them. (Fortunately RAND, which helped invent scenario forecasting, has a lot of experience at running such events, so no one tried to burn the other side's flag.)

Of course, anthropologists – or for that matter most people – have long known that identity is important. The utility of the outcome of a sports match will depend rather heavily on which team you associate with, the winner or the loser. Music fans often get as much pleasure from the sense of being part of something as they do from their favourite band's actual music. As discussed in the opening chapter, Brexit was as much about identity as it was about dry calculations of utility.

Under the influence

Identity economics shows how social norms influence our preferences; however, at an even more basic level, our understanding of the world is in large part shaped by people around us.

As discussed in earlier chapters, cognitive heuristics act as shortcuts, but they also act as a way to preserve our sense of self, and above all the belief that we are right. And being right often just means that the people around you agree with you. And the easiest way to achieve that, of course, is to agree with *them* in the first place.

According to cognitive scientist Steven Sloman, speaking in an interview with *Vox*, 'our attitudes are shaped much more by our social groups than they are by facts on the ground. We are not great reasoners. Most people don't like to think at all, or like to think as little as possible.' (Readers of *Hot Science* books are, of course, exceptions to this rule.)

An example is the hot-button issue of immigration, which was explored so thoroughly – but also to so little effect – in the Brexit debate. 'When I express an attitude about immigration, what am I really doing?' asks Sloman. 'I live in a very limited universe, and so I have to depend on the beliefs and knowledge of other people. I know what I've read; I know what I've heard from experts.' Instead of examining ideas or coming up with new ones, we prefer to spend our mental energy justifying our existing beliefs, which are shaped to some extent by our local circumstances, but even more by our social circle.

One result is that attitudes towards complex social issues tend to get hardened along group lines. Another, though, is that we can be quite easily manipulated. This was famously demonstrated by the psychologist Solomon Asch in a 1951 experiment, in which he asked subjects to perform a 'vision test' that involved looking at a line segment, and saying which of three other lines was closest to it in length. The test was done in a group which consisted of seven stooges and one actual subject. The stooges would go first and all give the same answer – one which was obviously wrong. About a third of the time, the subject would go against the evidence of their own eyes and agree with the group.

In other words, while what Kahneman calls our 'cognitive machinery' has a few bugs when running on its own, it can be completely overridden by the influence of other people.

Herd on the street

Humans are inherently social: we like the company of other people; but we also like to feel that we are making the right choices. This sets up a feedback loop, where our desire to join an emerging trend in turn magnifies that trend, thus affirming its correctness and making it more likely that others will join too.

Imagine, for example, that a restaurant opens for business, and for some random reason attracts quite a few customers in its first few weeks. A visitor walking by will be swayed to choose this restaurant if it looks full, just because that is an obvious sign that it must be reasonably good. Therefore the number of customers is amplified by positive feedback: the more customers there are, the more new ones will be generated. As business improves, the proprietor may invest the proceeds in more staff or advertising. The restaurant therefore pulls further ahead of its competition. Meanwhile, a restaurant down the road, which was just as good to start off with, quietly goes bust within a year or two – as most new businesses do.

The tendency for individuals to fall in line with the crowd is of course not unique to humans, but is shared by many animals. Cows herd, birds flock, wolves hunt in packs, fish swim in schools, wildebeest stampede in unison. From an evolutionary perspective, this might make sense, on the basis that there is safety – and efficiency – in numbers. An antelope might be able to access better grass by straying off the beaten path, but it would then have to spend much of its time with its head up looking for lions.

It is also much easier to see the consequences of an action if you watch someone else do it first. And if the aim is to be right, then it is also to avoid being wrong – and especially to avoid being the only one who is wrong.

Herd behaviour also gives us a different angle on the default effect – one reason we go for the default option is that presumably others are choosing it as well, which makes it seem safer. But sometimes this instinct to follow the crowd can get us into trouble. Perhaps the ultimate example of herd behaviour is the groupthink seen in cults. A less dramatic example is financial markets – which serve as a kind of Petri dish for behavioural biases. This brings us back to the topic of efficient markets.

Beauty contest

Fama's conception of an efficient market was a place where 'there are large numbers of rational profit maximizers actively competing, with each trying to predict future market values of individual securities, and where important current information is almost freely available to all participants'. However, in his 1936 *General Theory* Keynes compared the stock market

– in a rather different analogy – to a beauty contest, where people are asked to vote on which of a hundred photographs they think is the prettiest, and the game is to vote for the one which wins. 'It is not a case of choosing those which, to the best of one's judgment, are really the prettiest, nor even those which average opinion genuinely thinks the prettiest. We have reached the third degree where we devote our intelligences to anticipating what average opinion expects the average opinion to be. And there are some, I believe, who practise the fourth, fifth and higher degrees.' If an investor judges that a particular stock is well-liked by their peers, then it makes sense to buy that stock, which again acts as a feedback loop by increasing demand for the stock and boosting its price.

In the 1960s, the economist Hyman Minsky showed how these feedback loops create instability in the economy. While Minsky wouldn't have described himself as a behavioural economist, since the term hadn't been invented yet, his theory was driven by the need to include human psychology in economics. His 'instability hypothesis' was best summarised by the idea that 'stability is destabilizing'. When times are good, people relax and become confident in the future. They borrow money to make investments. As more people join the trend, those investments go up in value, and the perceived level of risk goes down. Banks are doing well and are increasingly eager to loan money to further boost their profits. This encourages more borrowing, and so on.

As the pattern becomes established, confidence grows into a feeling of exuberance. Fear of taking a risk is replaced by fear of missing out. The more you borrow, and the higher the leverage, the more you make. Speculation becomes a craze, never-ending growth is rationalised, and the few remaining sceptics are told that 'this time is different'.

The last people to join are what Minsky called the 'Ponzi' borrowers, who rely on capital growth in order to pay off their loans. But debt burdens are becoming unsustainable, and at some point the bubble starts to collapse. The first thing to go is liquidity, as sellers cling to their price anchors. Bankruptcies rise, forced sellers emerge, and banks tighten their lending standards. Exuberance is replaced by fear, then panic. Risk taking is replaced by loss avoidance. People cut back on spending, which feeds a broader economic decline. Finally, as the debt burden slowly shrinks, things start to recover. People remain cautious for a while, but the cycle soon repeats.

The business cycle is therefore not just a function of financial conditions, but an expression of psychological factors such as optimism bias, herd behaviour, and raw emotion. Indeed, the psychological and the financial are two sides of the same coin.

Something of an outsider in the economics profession, Minsky suggested three reasons why this psychology-driven instability was not taken seriously by economists. One was a version of present bias: government policies had done a fairly good job of stabilising the economy during the mid-twentieth century, so instability wasn't on the radar. Another was what Kahneman later called the illusion of control: economists thought they had a much better understanding of how the economy worked, so problems could be quickly fixed. Perhaps the greatest, though, was herd behaviour – among economists. As the economist Steven Pressman puts it: 'Infatuated with individual rationality, and at the same time behaving in a herd-like fashion, economists came to believe the efficient-market hypothesis.' Bubbles weren't just off-radar, they just couldn't happen.

In other words, efficient market theory was itself a version of a bubble, driven by herd behaviour and the desire for humans to both connect with each other and construct a consistent story that makes sense of reality.

Bubble trouble

Minsky died in 1996 so didn't live to see the financial crisis of 2007–8, but he would have recognised the script. His analysis of market psychology formed the foundation for the field of behavioural finance, and became particularly popular following the crisis. As Thaler points out, 'It also didn't hurt that financial markets offer the best opportunities to make money if markets are misbehaving, so a lot of intellectual resources have gone into investigating possible profitable investment strategies.'

Another behavioural expert to mine this seam was Robert Shiller, who met Thaler in 1982 and was convinced by him, as Thaler wrote, to 'embrace the heretical idea that social phenomena might influence stock prices as much as they do fashion trends. Hemlines go up and down without any reason; might not stock prices be influenced in other similar ways that seem to be beyond the standard economist's purview?'

If markets were really efficient, Shiller noted, then market changes should be driven only by news; and if there were no news, then the price should be stable. Yet empirical analysis showed that price changes often occur for no reason at all. Also, while prices were supposed to reflect an asset's intrinsic value, as measured by the discounted value of future dividends, his estimates showed that asset prices were much more volatile than were the future dividend streams. And finally there was the troubling issue of bubbles, which he described in his Nobel lecture as 'A situation in which news of price increases spurs investor enthusiasm which spreads by psychological contagion from person to person, in the process amplifying stories that might justify the price increase and bringing in a larger and larger class of investors, who, despite doubts about the real value of the investment, are drawn to it partly through envy of others' successes and partly through a gambler's excitement'.

Before leaving the question of financial instability, though, it should be noted that this instability is not caused solely by human psychology. Today, many trades are carried out not by humans, but by automated computer algorithms, whose response time is measured in microseconds. One unanticipated consequence is periodic flash crashes, where asset prices suddenly plunge for no apparent reason. These are often driven by algorithms which copy each other and create feedback loops between themselves.

This is ironic given that such computerised algorithms are designed to optimise short-term profit, and make decisions in a way that is impervious to human biases. They are therefore the closest thing we have to rational economic man. And yet, when they are brought into contact with one another, their net behaviour is as irrational as that of any human group. The reason is that markets are affected by the fragile and intrinsically uncertain link between price and value, which tends to elude and frustrate both man and machine.

Equally interesting, from a sociological perspective, is how the idea that 'social phenomena might influence stock prices' could possibly be described as 'heretical'. We return to this topic in the final chapter.

THE BIG PICTURE

8

In recent years, many ideas from behavioural economics have entered the mainstream. It is commonplace to think of people being nudged, either by government missives, or – and often to far greater effect – by things like advertisements or mobile apps. But as already discussed, the concept of nudging is very old, it just used to go by different names, like marketing or manipulation (see box below). And while behavioural psychologists have come up with a bewildering variety of cognitive biases, and have helped to understand phenomena such as financial crises, it is less clear what influence it has had on the way we think about the economy as a whole. This final chapter looks at the big picture of macroeconomics, considers the case against behavioural economics, and asks whether it really represents a new paradigm for economics.

Most of the behavioural effects we have encountered so far are related to questions of individual choice. Macroeconomics, in contrast, concerns issues which affect the economy as a whole, such as national productivity or employment rates.

The field, in its modern form, is usually said to have started with the publication by Keynes of his *General Theory* in 1936. Written during the Great Depression, its focus was on how to prevent future such events. Keynes argued that there is a disconnect between output, wages, and demand. When demand falls, wages do not adjust immediately because of what behavioural economists would call the anchor effect and loss aversion – workers refuse to accept a salary that is less than what they formerly earned. Companies therefore fire workers, resulting in unemployment. The 'animal spirits' of entrepreneurs are depressed, which leads to lower investment. The only way to get around this is for the government to ramp up spending to give the economy a boost.

While Keynes, though trained in mathematics, did not rely on mathematical models for his arguments, his ideas were gradually mathematicised in the mid-twentieth century by economists such as Paul Samuelson to create the so-called neoclassical synthesis. This was like the regular neoclassical economics, except that numerous 'frictions' were included to represent things like market failure, tax distortions, or bounded rationality. These acted as adjustments to the existing model, without challenging the fundamental assumption that markets – at least in their perfect and undistorted form – would drive prices to a stable equilibrium.

Meanwhile, another approach, called New Classical economics, led by Robert Lucas and Milton Friedman, argued that the neoclassical synthesis was insufficiently neoclassical because it still held out a role for government intervention, and suffered from a lack of mathematical rigour – rather than being based on sound 'microfoundations' such as rational economic man, the model featured numerous ad hoc adjustments. They therefore advocated a return to the rational utility-maximising model, based on a single representative agent who can see into the future and acts rationally to optimise his utility.

By the mid-1970s, mainstream academic economists had therefore bifurcated into two camps: the New Keynesians and the New Classicals. The former believed that unemployment should be addressed by government action; the latter believed that unemployment was a voluntary condition that occurred when people rationally decided to not accept current wages or working conditions. One was equilibrium postponed, the other was equilibrium now. But like two branches of a religious sect, they agreed on many things – including the idea that there was an equilibrium at all.

Behavioural economics and marketing

According to the marketing professor Philip Kotler, behavioural economics is 'another word for marketing'. It is true that many of the key ideas of behavioural economics have been known to marketers – if perhaps in a less scientific way – for about a century.

As an example, in his 1923 book *Crystallizing Public Opinion*, the public relations expert Edward Bernays described people as 'logic-proof', said that 'the group and herd are the basic mechanisms of public change', and argued that psychology could be used to manipulate the masses. His many successful campaigns included one in 1929 that persuaded women to smoke by calling cigarettes feminist 'Torches of Freedom'.

According to Bernays, 'psychological habits' – or what behavioural economists call cognitive biases – such as stereotyping 'are shorthand by which human effort is minimized'.

We are also subject to group influences: 'The tendency the group has to standardize the habits of individuals and to assign logical reasons for them is an important factor in the work of the public relations counsel ... The biological significance of homogeneity lies in its survival value. The wolf pack is many times as strong as the combined strength of each of its individual members.'

On the topic of fake news, Bernays wrote that, in relations with the press, the public relations counsellor 'is not merely the purveyor of news; he is more logically the creator of news'.

In another sense, though, perhaps behavioural economists have been the clever marketers. After all, they found a way to introduce behavioural psychology and marketing theory into economics, while respecting things like status quo bias.

The lion tamer

A key assumption in both the New Keynesian and New Classical approaches was that markets are fundamentally fair, and consumers have access to the same information. This assumption was questioned by George Akerlof in his 1970 paper on the market for 'lemons', i.e. secondhand cars of dubious quality. He argued that there was an information asymmetry between buyer and seller – the buyer knew the quality of the car, while the seller largely had to guess – and used this as an example to show how such asymmetry leads to problems in markets. While this was more a comment on market structure than on behavioural quirks, Akerlof described it in his 2001 Nobel lecture as 'a very first step toward the realization of a dream. That dream was the development of a behavioral macroeconomics in the original spirit of John Maynard Keynes' *General Theory*.'

According to Akerlof, the New Classical model in particular failed to explain a number of features of the real economy. These included (to paraphrase his lecture) the existence of involuntary unemployment; the impact of monetary policy on output and employment; the failure of deflation to accelerate when unemployment is high; the prevalence of undersaving for retirement; the excessive volatility of stock prices relative to their fundamentals; and the stubborn persistence of a self-destructive underclass.

Behavioural economics could address all of these problems. Indeed, 'If there is any subject in economics which should be behavioral, it is macroeconomics.'

Behavioural economists argued that *involuntary unemployment* occurred because, rather than employers lowering wages to hire as many workers as possible, they prefer to have fewer people working at a so-called 'efficiency wage' which acts as a motivational carrot, on the basis that it is better to have a few happy workers than many disgruntled ones. Meanwhile, those who are turned away are unwilling to accept worse-paying positions elsewhere because they anchor to their previous wages level, which serves as a reference point. According to Kahneman, 'the minimal wage that unemployed workers would accept for new employment averages 90% of their previous wage, and it drops by less than 10% over a period of one year.'

While according to neoclassical theory *monetary policy*

just changes the price level – so rational economic man discounts it – behavioural economists argued that it matters because prices are important psychologically – a boost in the money supply, for example, can lead to a real boost in output. Deflation during a recession is limited again by 'downward wage rigidity' which is 'a natural implication of prospect theory'.

People *undersave for retirement* because of things like inertia (they procrastinate on making the decision to save), loss aversion (they don't like a smaller pay packet), and lack of self-control in the face of present bias. Small changes such as making enrolment into employee retirement savings plans the default option – as companies such as the McDonald's hamburger chain did long before it was suggested by economists – or asking employees to commit to saving a proportion of future pay rises (which eliminates present bias and loss aversion) can significantly increase the rate of adoption. A 2014 study, based on observations of the saving behaviour of some 41 million Danish employees from 1995 to 2000, showed that changes in tax policy tended to affect only a minority of sophisticated active investors, which limited their effectiveness. The advantage of nudges is that they work also for the larger group of passive investors.

As discussed in the previous chapter, the apparent *irrationality of stock prices* can be explained by behavioural finance. Finally, while neoclassical theory associated poverty with levels of human and nonhuman capital, and struggled to explain *persistent poverty*, according to Akerlof the latter could be explained in part by identity economics – people in the underclass identify with the underclass, which is why they stay there. 'Since the prescriptions of the dominant culture endorse "self-fulfillment", those of the oppositional culture are self-destructive. The identity of the oppositional culture may be easier on the ego, but it is also likely to be economically and physically debilitating.'

Akerlof's lecture concluded by saying how economists had 'domesticated' Keynesian theory as they translated it into the mathematics of classical economics. 'But economies, like lions, are wild and dangerous. Modern behavioral economics has rediscovered the wild side of macroeconomic behavior. Behavioral economists are becoming lion tamers.'

How's it working out?

Akerlof's Nobel was awarded some two decades ago and, as we have seen, behavioural economics has made considerable progress since then in integrating itself into the mainstream. The issues highlighted in his talk have also become increasingly relevant, especially following the financial crisis of 2007–8, and the more recent coronavirus crisis of 2020.

In the US, for example, official unemployment numbers prior to the 2020 pandemic were about the same as they were in 2001, but the participation rate had gone down (by about 4 per cent), suggesting that many people have simply stopped looking for work. Post-pandemic is of course another story.

If monetary policy doesn't work, then no one told central bankers such as Ben Bernanke, or Akerlof's wife Janet Yellen, or current Federal Reserve chairman Jerome Powell, who came up with increasingly elaborate versions of it at the Fed in order to help restore the US economy to health. On the other hand, their attempts to fine-tune things like inflation seem a good example of the 'illusion of control', which again is the tendency to overrate the importance of our own actions as compared to other effects that are out of our control.

The idea that people will rationally save enough for retirement is currently being tested to destruction by the baby boomers, many of whom have no plans to retire. According to a 2016 analysis of 2013 data, the median working-age American couple has saved about $5,000 for retirement. This seems to make a mockery of the idea of rational economic man optimising his utility and that of his descendants into the infinite future.

Anyone who still thinks markets are self-stabilising won't be happy to hear that their tax dollars – or new money created from nothing by central banks – are what stabilise them after massive government bailouts for private companies. Worries about persistent poverty and the underclass have been complemented by worries about the middle class, which is shrinking in an era that rivals that of the robber barons in the 1930s for social inequality. CEO compensation, meanwhile, has ballooned, not because CEOs are responsible for a company's success (in fact there is little discernible benefit), but because they tend to get credit for it – the 'halo effect'.

In a way these developments vindicate the behavioural approach, but they also point to the fact that behavioural economists seem better at identifying problems than at implementing effective solutions. For example, behavioural economics and nudge theory were very influential during the Obama administration, but problems such as social inequality in the US only increased in that time. As journalist Hettie O'Brien wrote in the *New Statesman*, 'Rather than confronting the economic structures that create profound inequalities, nudges are designed to encourage people to cope with their material circumstances ... nudges have too often been a substitute for, rather than a complement to, ambitious intervention.'

Another example is the increasing popularity of statistical methods such as randomised controlled trials (RCTs). In medicine, an RCT compares outcomes for patients who receive different treatments with a control trial, which could be a standard treatment, a placebo, or no treatment at all. In recent decades the approach has been applied to other areas as well, including economics. The 2019 economics Nobel was awarded to the team of Michael Kremer, Abhijit Banerjee and Esther Duflo for their work using RCTs to find out which interventions are most effective at combating poverty in developing countries. For example, a 1990s experiment in rural Kenya found that handing out free textbooks and meals in schools did not improve educational outcomes. Other experiments in India showed that tutoring special-needs children did make a difference. Others found that parents in low-income countries are more likely to give their children deworming pills if those pills are free, as opposed to heavily subsidised.

The 'randomistas', as they are known, have helped introduce the phrase 'evidence based' into economics, which is a good thing. At the same time, RCTs are no panacea. In medicine they are used to get regulatory approval for drugs, but finding cures for cancer – or overcoming the structural problems which underlie world poverty – will certainly require more radical thinking.

So what can behavioural economics tell us about other key economic issues which have received increasing attention, including societal happiness, gender relations, and climate change? And is behavioural economics effective as a policy tool, or is it being used as a sticking plaster to avoid more difficult therapies?

Feeling happy

Starting with the topic of societal happiness, according to neoclassical theory this is obtained by maximising utility. It can therefore be expressed using money-based metrics such as a person's net worth, or a country's gross domestic product. Behavioural economists complement this approach with the rather more direct technique of asking people in surveys how happy they are.

One problem with such surveys is that, as we have seen, the answers are affected by context. For example, one experiment started off by asking a group of students about their dating life, if they had gone out last night, and if so how that went. They then asked how happy the student was. The students who had enjoyed the previous night tended to report a higher level of happiness. This effect mostly disappeared with another group, who were asked to report their happiness first. The order of the questions therefore affected the response. In fact, this 'order effect' is a very common phenomenon, as survey writers know.

Another complication is that happiness is partially genetic, and partially adaptive. Our general level of happiness is largely a function of character, so changes tend to be transient. At the same time, while events such as an accident or winning a lottery can change our level of happiness for a while, we soon adapt to our new circumstances, so they affect us only when we are thinking about them, which isn't much of the time (chronic conditions such as depression being an exception).

There is also a difference between happiness as experienced and recorded through the course of a typical day, and our general level of satisfaction with how life is going. The former – which Kahneman calls a 'hedonimeter total', echoing Edgeworth – will be affected by how much time we spend doing pleasant and unpleasant things, so depends on an experience's duration. Commuting to work is not the same as a walk in the park (unless you are very lucky), and an hour commute is worse than a half-hour commute.

Reported life satisfaction is more of a story that you are telling yourself, and is affected by factors such as peak or most recent experiences, or whether you have lived up to your expectations. One experiment over a 20-year timescale showed that teenagers who described their goal as 'becoming accomplished in a performing art' had the lowest life satisfaction as adults. As with cognition, or with eyesight, what we see depends on what we focus on, and where we draw the frame. In one study by Kahneman and the economist Angus Deacon, the authors concluded 'that high income buys life satisfaction but not happiness, and that low income is associated with both low life evaluation and low emotional well-being'.

Finally, an important component of happiness is a sense of control over one's life – and unlike wealth, power is a zero-sum game. Even if everyone gets richer, there will still be people at the bottom who feel they are being exploited.

From an economic perspective, perhaps the biggest message is that economic growth does not necessarily lead to a state of greater reported happiness. Of course, this seems obvious, since otherwise our ancestors must have been very depressed; but it does somewhat undercut the notion from neoclassical economics that things like income and net worth measure utility and are therefore necessarily good.

Gender relations

The field of feminist economics has existed as a subdiscipline in its own right since at least 1988, when Marilyn Waring published *If Women Counted: A New Feminist Economics*. A longstanding criticism of mainstream economics was that it was based on a fundamentally gendered view of the world, and ignored or downplayed the unpaid contributions of people outside the workforce, of whom most happened to be women. As the anthropologist Mary Catherine Bateson noted, 'The dangerous idea that lies behind "economic man" is the idea that anyone can be entirely rational or entirely self-interested. One of the corollaries, generally unspoken in economics texts, was that such clarity could not be expected of women who were liable to be distracted by such things as emotions or concern for others.'

Feminist economics remained on the fringes of academic economics until after the 2007–8 crisis, when it was shown that the effects of austerity programs and the crisis itself impacted women more than men – in the UK for example they bore an estimated 85 per cent of the brunt. This asymmetry was related to another one, which was gender bias within the profession itself. A study comparing gender balance in different academic fields concluded that 'Economics is an outlier, with a persistent sex gap in promotion that cannot be readily explained by productivity differences.' During a 2019 panel discussion on gender issues, Janet Yellen even said that addressing the issue of sex discrimination 'should be the highest priority' for economists.

So why is it that, in the words of sociologist Elaine Coburn, 'mainstream economics remains remarkably "pre-feminist"'? One reason, perhaps, is that economics maintains an illusion of objectivity and rationality, where complex social issues such as power and gender are ignored or downplayed. As Yellen said of her male colleagues, 'I think they regard themselves as rational and the field as being highly meritocratic.' However, that stance is just another form of cognitive bias. It will be an interesting experiment in behavioural psychology to see how the field of economics changes as it becomes more diverse (which I am assuming will happen since it couldn't be much less diverse).

Climate crisis

Climate change seems another problem that behavioural economics might help address – especially since using conventional techniques such as logic doesn't seem to be working. Present bias, for example, means that people are more likely to see global warming as a problem if they are asked on a warm day. Confirmation bias (where we seek out information which supports our views) means that the climate debate becomes increasingly polarised. And the 'shifting baseline effect' means that we don't notice things like the warming climate, or the collapse in insect numbers, because they are happening slowly as compared to the timescales of our own lives. We forget, or aren't old enough to remember, that a drive through the country used to result in rather more dead bugs on the windscreen; we adjust to each new 'extreme weather event' so that they no longer seem extreme.

Tools such as carbon taxes can be viewed as a way of nudging people into reducing their carbon footprint. However, even these nudges meet with resistance. One 2019 poll found that 'Canadians are deeply concerned about climate change and are willing to make adjustments in their lives to fight it – but for many people, paying as much as even a monthly Netflix subscription in extra taxes is not one of them.'

One small change that can make a difference is to use different words. In 2019 the company SPARK Neuro set out, according to its website, 'to find out if it's time to rebrand climate change'. They did this by using electroencephalography (EEG) measurements of electrical activity in the brain, along with galvanic skin response (GSR) recordings, to gauge the emotional intensity of subjects' responses as they listened to audio recordings of different phrases. It turned out that 'global warming' and 'climate change' elicited little in the way of sweaty palms or brain activity, while phrases involving the words 'crisis', 'destruction', 'destabilisation' and 'collapse' did better.

Again, though, if behavioural economists wish to change our approach to economics, a good place to start is with mainstream economics itself, which, as many environmentalists point out, has probably done more to impede action against climate change (sorry, the climate crisis) than to assist it, by long prioritising economic growth above all else, even if lip service is paid to 'market failures' such as pollution. And while the idea of 'nudging' can be effective for some problems, the reality is that small-scale nudges can actually distract us from the need to implement serious reforms, which go beyond presentation or branding.

As mentioned in Chapter 2, Thaler wrote after visiting the UK Conservative Party in 2008 that the behavioural approach 'was one that the party could support as part of a rebranding that Cameron and Osborne were undertaking. Their stated goal was to make the party more progressive and pro-environment.' But one suspects their real goal was to rebrand the party so it *looked* more progressive and pro-environment, while launching an austerity program that would make severe cuts to public services, including health (relevant for the next section) and environmental agencies (relevant for the environment). The main contribution of the Cameron government's Nudge team to combating climate change was to notice that some homeowners weren't installing loft insulation because their lofts were a mess, even though government subsidies were available. So, to make it easier, they suggested adding an option, at extra expense, where companies installing the insulation could help to clean out the loft. However the policy was not actually adopted.

Cass Sunstein noted that 'Default rules of various sorts (say, double-sided printing) can promote environmental protection.' But contrast such nudges with the approach of people like the teenage climate activist Greta Thunberg. She doesn't gently prod people into change, or make it sound easy – she gives speeches that challenge, confront, and disrupt. The protest group called Extinction Rebellion, which has organised strikes and demonstrations around the world, does not employ clever behavioural techniques, it shuts down city centres. And if things like forest fires or melting ice caps don't nudge people into action, then nor will subtle rewording, or finely tuned incentives.

Wash your hands

The limitations of nudging as a policy tool were highlighted in 2020 by the COVID-19 pandemic. In a Bloomberg piece published 28 February that year, Sunstein – who does not apparently possess expertise in epidemiology, or for that matter a crystal ball – counselled that any spread of the disease 'will induce much more fear, and much more in the way of economic and social dislocation, than is warranted by the actual risk. Many people will take precautionary steps (cancelling vacations, refusing to fly, avoiding whole nations) even if there is no adequate reason to do that. Those steps can in turn increase economic dislocations, including plummeting stock prices … the best response to excessive fear is to put the issue of probability on people's view screens, and to do so directly and explicitly.'

Unfortunately, the 'issue of probability' that Sunstein was talking about turned out to be the wrong kind of probability. Pandemics don't follow a gentle 'additive' kind of probability distribution, with a well-defined average amenable to statistical modelling; instead they follow a multiplicative probability, where effects that start small can quickly grow out of control. And as with the climate system, they are shaped by powerful feedback loops which make accurate prediction impossible.

While Sunstein's advice may not have been responsible for Donald Trump's initial 'hunch' that the virus would turn out to be no worse than a flu, the behavioural approach was taken more seriously in the UK, where the response to the pandemic was shaped by the Scientific Advisory Group for Emergencies (SAGE), a revolving panel with about 20 members. Attendees at SAGE meetings happened to include the main architects of Brexit: Johnson's Chief Adviser Dominic Cummings (whose university degree was in history), and the data scientist Ben Warner, whom the *Sunday Times* once described as the 'Leave campaign's data geek'. The group did feature experts on topics such as the mathematical modelling of pandemics, but had no immunologists, molecular virologists, or intensive care experts with more hands-on experience. On the other hand it did have two behavioural scientists and input from people including psychologist David Halpern, head of the Nudge Unit.

Following a 9 March SAGE report on 'behavioural and social interventions', Halpern told the BBC that the strategy was to protect at-risk groups by isolating them. 'By the time they come out of their cocooning, herd immunity has been achieved in the rest of the population.' Putting the economy into lockdown would only invite what he called 'behavioural fatigue' (although other behavioural economists later described behavioural fatigue as 'a nebulous concept').

As Bloomberg reported on 11 March, 'A little-known team of advisers specializing in behavioral psychology is helping to steer the prime minister's response to the health crisis, shunning headline measures like travel restrictions and quarantines to focus on a more banal task: finding ways to persuade people to wash their hands.' According to Halpern, 'A lot of people don't wash their hands very often', so the aim was to create a 'behavioral scaffolding to form a new habit'.

In what looks like a clear demonstration of optimism bias, 'Johnson's team insisted there was no need to test him', even after his junior health minister was diagnosed with coronavirus, 'because they hadn't been in close contact and he regularly washes his hands'. Johnson – who just days before had bragged that 'I was at a hospital the other night where I think there were actually a few coronavirus patients and I shook hands with everybody' – even announced that he had stopped shaking hands, because 'The behavioral psychologists say that if you don't shake somebody's hand then that sends an important message to them about the importance of washing your hands.'

Obviously, the idea that the pandemic could be handled by gently nudging people towards good personal hygiene was hugely attractive to Johnson. After all, shutting down the economy wasn't exactly in the spirit of Brexit. At the same time, what Bloomberg called the 'Keep Calm And Wash Your Hands' approach was 'still a gamble for Johnson. If locking down millions of people proves successful elsewhere, and the virus spreads uncontrollably across Britain, the policy will look like a terrible mistake.'

Just as Cameron had gambled on behavioural psychology with Brexit, Johnson was doing something similar with a microbe. The country would once again be immune to 'Project Fear'! However, his policy flew in the face of advice from scientists with more direct experience of pandemics, and COVID-19 in particular, who put more emphasis on things like testing, adequate equipment, and early lockdown.

Indeed, the countries with the most success in tackling the crisis relied not on nudges, but on speedy implementation of such measures. As the *Lancet*'s Richard Horton observed, 'When the government realised that a new virus was circulating, Chinese officials didn't advise hand washing, a better cough etiquette and disposing of tissues. They quarantined entire cities and shut down the economy.' In New Zealand, while the UK's SAGE was musing over behavioural scaffolding, Prime Minister Jacinda Ardern decided to 'go hard and go early'. She imposed a fourteen-day quarantine on anyone entering the country on 14 March, and implemented a strict lockdown two weeks later, before anyone had died. As Greta Thunberg observed, the results provided evidence that 'during a crisis you act with necessary force'.

The UK finally reversed its policy and announced a late lockdown on 23 March, after 335 deaths, and four days before Johnson was himself diagnosed with coronavirus. Poll results showed six weeks later that, far from suffering from 'behavioural fatigue', only one in five of a frightened and suddenly highly risk-averse populace were ready for the restrictions on schools, pubs and restaurants to be relaxed.

Time will tell which policies have the best long-term outcomes – if no vaccine or treatment is forthcoming, it could well be that an excessive lockdown just pushes the problem down the road – but what seems clear is that the reaction to the crisis in the UK was delayed, confused and ineffective. One problem, Horton noted, was that the scientists 'suffered from a "cognitive bias" towards the milder threat of influenza' and thought 'we could have a controlled epidemic' (illusion of control). Another expert with inside knowledge of its working practices accused SAGE of suffering from 'groupthink'.

Of course, there are real questions over how best to encourage social and personal habits and norms that will limit transmission, and behavioural approaches have an important part to play. But one wonders if an excessive emphasis on such approaches has itself become a cognitive bias, that should be added to the list – and whether the best way to address it would be to go back to the old-fashioned kinds of experts, who actually know about a relevant speciality.

The basic problem, it seems, is that some things – from a virus to the climate system – do not respond well to subtle psychological adjustments on our part. Instead, they are giving us a 'nudge' of their own. While the exact source of the virus is debated, many researchers believe that the increasing encroachment of human activity into natural systems enhances the probability of microbes jumping the species barrier and creating dangerous new pathogens. Together with equally unsubtle signals from the climate system (forest fires, melting glaciers, etc.), such outbreaks could be the planet's way of telling us that our present economic system is unsustainable.

Behavioural economics could in principle be part of the solution, by helping to unwind the neoclassical model and pointing to alternatives – but instead of challenging existing ideas or power structures, it is too often about rebranding and increasing compliance, whether it is for retirement plans, parking tickets, tax returns, austerity measures, or washing your hands. For governments, the main attraction of behavioural economics often appears to be that it provides a useful cover for policies which deflect responsibility for things like a functioning social safety net away from those governments onto individuals. If ageing boomers aren't retiring in style – or worse, are dying because of coronavirus – it is because of cognitive defects. The state can wash its hands.

In the same way, instead of offering a radical alternative to mainstream economics, confronting that discipline's grave failings, behavioural economics is giving it a gentle and respectful nudge. However, it is becoming increasingly obvious that problems such as financial instability, widening inequality, pandemics, climate change and so on – all of which involve the economy and are affected by economic ideas – need something bolder and more urgent in order to address them. So does behavioural economics have a future, or will 'behavioural' go the way of countless other economic fads and labels? And how should we assess the contribution of behavioural approaches to the history of economic thought?

Renegade-lite

Behavioural economists certainly faced an enormous challenge in confronting the strongly held tenets of neoclassical economics. As money manager Jeremy Grantham wrote to his clients in 2009: 'Never underestimate the power of a dominant academic idea to choke off competing ideas, and never underestimate the unwillingness of academics to change their views in the face of evidence. They have decades of their research and their academic standing to defend.' As behavioural economist Matthew Rabin notes, though, Kahneman and Tversky's prospect theory also succeeded in part because 'they were able and willing to address economists in standard language and venues' which helps create a feeling of what Kahneman called 'cognitive ease'. And instead of saying that economists had to forget their assumptions of rational human behaviour, they said they just needed to add some more, thus avoiding loss aversion. Meanwhile, economists and policymakers alike are cast in the role of those who – with the help of behavioural economists and consultants – can see through, and manipulate, cognitive effects.

Behavioural economics has long cultivated an aura of being rebellious and outside the mainstream. But the barriers that the field confronted seem a little overstated. In his book *Misbehaving*, Thaler describes himself in a number of places as a 'renegade' and his work as 'heretical' or 'high treason'. 'Radical, troublemaker, rabble-rouser, nuisance, and other terms unsuitable for the printed page were all commonly used adjectives.' However, he wasn't exactly burned at the stake, or even, for that matter, apparently exposed at any point to a severe career setback. As the economist John Cochrane noted in a blog review, 'complaining about being ignored and mistreated is a bit unseemly for a Distinguished Service professor with a multiple-group low-teaching appointment at the very University of Chicago he derides, partner in an asset management company running $3 billion dollars, recipient of numerous awards including AEA vice president, and so on.'

This might sound like sniping between academics, but it matters because the rebel attitude is part of the sales pitch for behavioural economics. The fact that the approach has been largely accepted, or at least tolerated, by many academic economists – not to mention the Nobel committee – strengthens the mainstream, by making it appear more flexible and pluralistic than it actually is (heterodox economists find it hard even to publish in leading journals). This signalling of openness was especially needed after the 2007–8 crisis brought the entire profession of economics into question. Behavioural methods have also helped extend the economics approach into areas such as psychology, sociology, law, and so on in what economist Ariel Rubinstein compared to 'academic imperialism'.

However, the notion that something like nudging could be considered 'heretical' seems quaint in a time when the business model of social media companies is centred on addiction. And the reality is that behavioural economics looks less like a genuine paradigm shift than an adjustment to the existing classical paradigm. The fact that it modifies the existing classical model, rather than challenging it on a more fundamental level, is what has enabled it to succeed, but also limits its power.

For example, behavioural approaches have had only tangential influence on areas such as macroeconomics. As the *Oxford Review of Economic Policy*'s 'Rebuilding Macroeconomic Theory' project put it in 2018, the 'two critical assumptions' underpinning mainstream macroeconomic models are 'the efficient market hypothesis, and rational expectations'. While it recommends 'relaxing the requirement of rational expectations', it also remarks that 'there is not yet a new paradigm in sight'. Given the report was written some four decades after behavioural economics was invented, this seems unimpressive.

Behavioural economics seems to be following the pattern set by Keynes, whereby, as noted above, his ideas about human behaviour were mathematicised and made compatible with mainstream economics, but only in a very 'domesticated' form, as Akerlof put it. It can thus be treated as what one paper called 'an extra limb that extends the theory's reach to some anomalous behavior'. Or as another put it, behavioural economics 'extends rational choice and equilibrium models; it does not advocate abandoning these models entirely'. The aim is to 'modify one or two assumptions in standard theory in the direction of greater psychological realism' and thus avoid exciting too much in the way of status quo bias.

To take an even longer perspective, neoclassical economists spent a century stripping emotion and psychology from their field, only for behavioural economists to attempt to add it gingerly back in, while making sure not to overly disturb the existing structure. Instead of utility we have a modified value function; instead of Edgeworth's hedonimeter to measure our reactions, we have new and improved tools from neuroscientists. However, given the widespread acknowledgement that the status quo has failed, it seems that something more basic is called for.

Preference reversal II

Ultimately, the problem for any mathematical theory of human behaviour is that people do not behave like classical machines, obey classical logic, or follow classical probability. As an example, consider the problem of preference reversal. This, again, is the phenomenon, discussed in Chapter 5, where people change their mind over some question depending on the exact context. If subjects are presented with two lotteries, with different odds and payoffs, they might think the first is more valuable if the idea is to sell tickets to someone else, but actually prefer the second if the idea is to play themselves.

Preference reversal is usually demonstrated using controlled experiments, but it occurs all the time in economic life. A graphic illustration was provided by the observed rate of strategic default during the US housing crisis.

According to objective utility maximisation, it makes sense for a person to default on their mortgage and walk away if the costs associated with staying in the home exceed the costs associated with default. Surveys also indicated that homeowners were ready to default if this were the case.

However, when house prices actually did decline dramatically, and homeowners were faced with a real choice, their preferences reversed rather dramatically. Nearly always, people opted to stay in their homes as long as possible, even if it made no financial sense.

In fact, the Federal Reserve found in a report that the 'median borrower walks away from his home when he is 62 percent underwater'. Viewed another way, this means that the cost of staying in the current home was about two and a half times the cost of buying a similar replacement at depressed prices.

The reason for the preference reversal is of course that subjective feelings such as guilt over default, and fear of the possible consequences, tend to be more strongly experienced when making an actual potentially life-altering decision than when completing a survey for a researcher. However, because the effect depends on context, it eludes classical treatment, and can only be addressed in behavioural economics by building an ad hoc model.

Indeed, as discussed in Chapter 5, behavioural models struggle to explain a number of cognitive phenomena, including the Ellsberg paradox with its uncertainty aversion, or the disjunction effect where reasons for a particular choice seem to cancel each other out when they are both present, or the order effect where our response to questions depends on the order in which they are presented. While these are often framed as puzzles or paradoxes, they go to the root of human behaviour and have very real effects.

The problem ultimately is that decisions involve both objective and subjective factors, but these don't seem to add together in the usual way, and the result is dependent on context. Viewed this way, the value function and the uncertainty function of prospect theory are tweaks to the straight lines of expected utility theory. They resemble the epicycles that the ancient astronomers added to their models when the movements of the planets defied their predictions.* These early astronomical models did not question the central idea that the planets move around the Earth in circles, but addressed the problem by adding extra complications – circles around circles. Similarly, prospect theory is more complicated than expected utility theory, and addresses many of its drawbacks, but it doesn't question the central idea that utility can or should be calculated using classical equations.

And while behavioural economics paints a more nuanced picture of human behaviour than does rational economic man, it is also firmly rooted in the idea of man as a predictable machine. Kahneman, for example, speaks of 'the design of the machinery of cognition'. Cognitive heuristics belong to what he and Tversky called the 'human information processing machinery that cannot be changed'. The aim is always to show that we are 'predictably irrational', as in the 2008 book of that name by Dan Ariely.

So perhaps instead of finding tweaks to standard utility theory, we need to use a different kind of mathematics, that can better accommodate the complex and often incompatible natures of objective and subjective effects. Fortunately, a more suitable framework exists already, and was developed by none other than the founder of utility theory, John von Neumann.

---

* Compare the images at: https://upload.wikimedia.org/wikipedia/commons/6/65/Cognitive_bias_codex_en.svg; https://upload.wiki media.org/wikipedia/commons/0/0e/Cassini_apparent.jpg

How much

Some eight years before publishing his *Theory of Games and Economic Behaviour* with Oskar Morgenstern, von Neumann co-authored a paper with Garrett Birkhoff on 'The Logic of Quantum Mechanics'. The object of the paper was 'to discover what logical structure one may hope to find in physical theories which, like quantum mechanics, do not conform to classical logic'.

The main feature of this quantum framework is that it describes a system not in terms of classical probabilities, but instead by amplitudes of a probabilistic wave function. Measurements involve a 'collapse' of the system to a certain state, so states where the wave amplitude is large have a higher change of being measured. Because waves in superposition can reinforce or subtract from each other, and are affected by context, it means that two factors might add together in one situation, but cancel out in another. And rather than being completely separate and independent, entities are entangled with each other and with the environment, so a change in one part affects the entire system.

Quantum probability can therefore be viewed as a more general version of probability, which allows for things like interference and entanglement. The development of the theory was prompted by the discoveries of physicists, but it could equally have been developed by mathematicians. Indeed, many of its tools had already been invented by mathematicians such as David Hilbert before they were adopted by physicists.

As computer scientist Scott Aaronson points out, quantum logic is 'about information and probabilities and observables, and how they relate to each other'. And researchers are increasingly finding that it applies as much to human interactions as it does to subatomic ones. An example is the above-mentioned disjunction effect, which can be attributed to a kind of mental interference that, as researchers Jerome Busemeyer and Peter Bruza note, 'is analogous to wave interference where two waves meet with one wave rising while the other wave is falling so they cancel out'.

Quantum models have been similarly built for a range of cognitive games and phenomena, from the prisoner's dilemma to the order effect, with considerable success. As the political scientist Alexander Wendt wrote in his 2015 book *Quantum Mind and Social Science*, 'the situation in cognitive science today seems similar to physics in the early 1900s. In both domains rigorous testing of classical theories had produced a string of anomalies; efforts to explain them with new classical models were ad hoc and partial; and then a quantum theory emerged that predicted them all with great precision.'

An empirical example is the above-mentioned episode of preference reversal, where homeowners elected to stay in their homes rather than default. A simple quantum model predicted (actually 'postdicted', since it was after the event) that the cost of staying in the home should be about three times the cost of defaulting before owners would choose the latter option, which, given the complexity of the problem, is in striking agreement with the value observed. When it comes to such decisions, people don't respond to subtle cues or finely judged incentives, but only to large and abrupt changes – the opposite of what is predicted or suggested by either neoclassical economics or nudge theory.

As researchers in the area of quantum finance have pointed out, the quantum approach seems particularly appropriate for the description of markets, where the price of something like a house or a stock is best described as a probabilistic wave function which 'collapses' to a particular price only during a transaction. And as I argued in my book *Quantum Economics: The New Science of Money*, the behaviour of money – with its sudden jumps, and its entanglements between debtor and creditor – is best handled using quantum mathematics.

Of course, social systems can never be reduced to a set of equations, quantum or otherwise, because they are complex systems with emergent properties that will always evade perfect computation. The same is true in physics – matter may ultimately be based on quantum interactions, but meteorologists don't use quantum models to predict the weather. However, the reason the quantum approach is now being adopted in many areas of social science is because it seems to be the right mathematical framework for addressing a range of problems, from individual decision-making, to the movements of the stock market, to international relations.

Indeed, the interesting question is not so much why quantum mathematics is now being applied outside physics, as why it took so long. Perhaps the reason is that, unlike behavioural economics, it challenges the most basic tenets of classical logic which underpin much of the Western worldview – in particular the idea, which goes back to the ancient Greeks, that a statement cannot be both true and false at the same time.

Classical computers, for example, are based on 'bits' which take on the value of 0 or 1. Quantum computers use 'qubits' which can exist in a superposition of 0 and 1 – they are both at the same time – which is what leads to effects such as interference. Much of the current interest in quantum finance – and quantum social science in general – is driven by the advent of quantum computing, with banks and start-ups vying to produce quantum algorithms to model and predict, not the bubbles, but the quantum foam of markets. A side-effect might be to change our view of how the economy works.

The axioms of choice

Quantum economics and finance is still in its early stages, and if the quantum approach does succeed, it will be in no small part due to the efforts of behavioural psychologists and behavioural economists, who pointed out the flaws in the basic principles of classical theory. And either way, any student or person interested in economics has much to learn from behavioural economics. This is especially the case given that theories of economics have a way of feeding back into the economy, and the behavioural view of the economy has already influenced the behaviour of governments, corporations, and individuals.

Perhaps the biggest contribution of behavioural economics is its emphasis on empirical evidence and data. As Thaler points out, 'most of economic theory is not derived from empirical observation. Instead, it is deduced from axioms of rational choice, whether or not those axioms bear any relation to what we observe in our lives every day.' Techniques such as surveys, controlled experiments, natural experiments (e.g. Brexit), online experiments, randomised trials, and the findings of neuroscience – coupled with huge increases in analytical ability in the age of big data – have changed the way economics is done, and behavioural economists both helped drive this change and were among the first to benefit from its application.

The axioms (from the Greek *axioma*, for 'that which is thought worthy or fit') of rational choice, which John von Neumann codified in the 1930s, have probably done more to shape human behaviour than any other mathematical model. But, as the poet John Keats wrote in a letter, 'Axioms in philosophy are not axioms until they are proved upon our pulses.' In other words, we have to feel them to be true. Fast forward to now, and we are seeing the consequences of these axioms. Behavioural economics is a vital step in releasing us from their constraints, and pointing the way towards a different and more humanistic kind of economics.

FURTHER READING

Chapter 1: Stay or Go?

Buchanan, T. (2019), 'Brexit Behaviourally: Lessons Learned from the 2016 Referendum', *Mind & Society*, 18: 13–31

Kahneman, D. (2011), *Thinking, Fast and Slow*, New York: Farrar, Straus and Giroux.

Levitt, S., and Dubner, S. (2005), *Freakonomics: A Rogue Economist Explores the Hidden Side of Everything*, New York: William Morrow.

Thaler, R.H. (2015), *Misbehaving: The Making of Behavioral Economics*, New York: W.W. Norton & Company.

Yeung, K. (2017), '"Hypernudge": Big Data as a Mode of Regulation by Design', *Information, Communication & Society*, 20(1): 118–136.

Chapter 2: The Rational(ish) Animal

Edgeworth, F.Y. (1881), *Mathematical Psychics: An Essay on the Application of Mathematics to the Moral Sciences*, London: C.K. Paul.

James, W. (1884), 'What is an Emotion?' *Mind*, 9(34): 188–205.

Jevons, W.S. (1957), *The Theory of Political Economy*, 5th edn, New York: Kelley & Millman.

Mauss, I.B., and Robinson, M.D. (2009), 'Measures of Emotion: A Review', *Cognition & Emotion*, 23(2): 209–237.

Orrell, D. (2017), *Economyths: 11 Ways Economics Gets It Wrong*, London: Icon Books.

Robbins, L. (1932), *An Essay on the Nature and Significance of Economic Science*, London: Macmillan.

Tomer, J.F. (2017), *Advanced Introduction to Behavioral Economics*. Cheltenham, UK: Edward Elgar Publishing.

Von Neumann, J., and Morgenstern, O. (1944), *Theory of Games and Economic Behavior*, Princeton, NJ: Princeton University Press.

Chapter 3: Too Much Information

Chabris, C.F., and Simons, D.J. (2010), *The Invisible Gorilla; or, Why You Have No Idea How Your Mind Works*, London: HarperCollins.

Iyengar, S.S., and Lepper, M.R. (2000), 'When Choice is Demotivating: Can One Desire Too Much of a Good Thing?', *Journal of Personality and Social Psychology*, 79(6), 995–1006.

Kahneman, D., and Tversky, A. (1973), 'On the Psychology of Prediction', *Psychological Review*, 80(4): 237–251.

Kahneman, D., and Tversky, A. (1974), 'Judgment Under Uncertainty: Heuristics and Biases', *Science*, 185(4157): 1124–1131.

Tversky, A., and Kahneman, D. (1983), 'Extension Versus Intuitive Reasoning: The Conjunction Fallacy in Probability Judgment', *Psychological Review*, 90(4): 293–315.

Northcraft, G.B., and Neale, M.A. (1987), 'Experts, Amateurs, and Real Estate: An Anchoring-and-Adjustment Perspective on Property Pricing Decisions', *Organizational Behavior and Human Decision Processes*, 39(1): 84–97.

Orrell, D., (2012), *Truth or Beauty: Science and the Quest for Order*, New Haven, CT: Yale University Press.

Schrage, M. (2003), 'Daniel Kahneman: The Thought Leader Interview', *Strategy+Business*, Winter 2003.

Simon, H. (1978), 'Rational Decision-Making in Business Organizations', Prize Lecture, available from: https://www. nobelprize.org/prizes/economic-sciences/1978/simon/lecture/

Chapter 4: Prospect Theory

Kahneman, D., and Tversky, A. (1979), 'Prospect Theory: An Analysis of Decision under Risk', *Econometrica*, 47(2): 263–291. This was based on a 1977 report, written as part of the US Department of Defense's Advanced Decision Technology Program, that is available from: https://apps.dtic.mil/dtic/tr/ fulltext/u2/a045771.pdf

Sieroń, A. (2020), 'Does the COVID-19 Pandemic Refute Probability Neglect?', *Journal of Risk Research* (in press).

Samuelson, W., and Zeckhauser, R. (1988), 'Status Quo Bias in Decision Making', *Journal of Risk and Uncertainty*, 1: 7–59.

Kahneman, D., Knetsch, J.L., Thaler, R.H. (1991), 'Anomalies: The Endowment Effect, Loss Aversion, and Status Quo Bias', *The Journal of Economic Perspectives*, 5(1): 193–206.

Kahneman, D. (2002), 'Daniel Kahneman – Biographical', retrieved from Nobelprize.org: https://www.nobelprize. org/nobel_prizes/economic-sciences/laureates/2002/ kahneman-bio.html

Chapter 5: 'Paradoxes'

Camerer, C., Babcock, L., Loewenstein, G., Thaler, R. (1997), 'Labor Supply of New York City Cabdrivers: One Day at a Time', *Quarterly Journal of Economics*, 112(2): 407–441.

Cohn, A., Fehr, E., Maréchal, M. (2014), 'Business Culture and Dishonesty in the Banking Industry', *Nature*, 516: 86–89.

Doyen, S., Klein, O., Pichon, C.-L., Cleeremans, A. (2012), 'Behavioral Priming: It's All in the Mind, but Whose Mind?', *PLoS ONE*, 7(1): e29081.

Thaler, R.H., and Sunstein, C.R. (2008), *Nudge: Improving Decisions about Health, Wealth, and Happiness*, New Haven: Yale University Press.

Tversky, A., and Kahneman, D. (1981), 'The Framing of Decisions and the Psychology of Choice', *Science*, 211(4481): 453–458.

Tversky, A., and Thaler, R.H. (1990), 'Anomalies: Preference Reversals', *Journal of Economic Perspectives*, 4: 201–11.

Vohs, K.D., Mead, N., Goode, M. (2006), 'The Psychological Consequences of Money', *Science*, 314: 1154–6.

Chapter 6: The Pleasure Machine

Ainslie, G.W. (1974), 'Impulse Control in Pigeons', *Journal of the Experimental Analysis of Behavior*, 21: 485–489.

Ariely, D., and Loewenstein, G. (2006), 'The Heat of the Moment: The Effect of Sexual Arousal on Sexual Decision Making', *Journal of Behavioral Decision Making*, 19(2): 87–98.

Briñol, P., and Petty, R.E. (2003), 'Overt Head Movements and Persuasion: A Self-Validation Analysis', *Journal of Personality and Social Psychology*, 84(6), 1123–1139.

Davies, S. (2019), 'Women's Minds Matter', *Aeon*. Available from: https://aeon.co/essays/feminists-never-bought-the-idea-of-a-mind-set-free-from-its-body

Loewenstein, G. (2000), 'Emotions in Economic Theory and Economic Behavior', *American Economic Review*, 90(2): 426–432.

McGilchrist, I. (2009), *The Master and his Emissary*, London: Yale University Press.

McGilchrist, I. (2010), 'Reciprocal Organization of the Cerebral Hemispheres', *Dialogues in Clinical Neuroscience*, 12(4), 503–515.

Mischel, W., Ebbesen, E.B., Raskoff Zeiss, A. (1972), 'Cognitive and Attentional Mechanisms in Delay of Gratification', *Journal of Personality and Social Psychology*, 21(2): 204–218.

Sacré, P., et al. (2019), 'Risk-taking Bias in Human Decision-making is Encoded via a Right–Left Brain Push–Pull system', *Proceedings of the National Academy of Sciences*, 116(4): 1404–1413.

Sunstein, C.R. (2017), *Human Agency and Behavioral Economics: Nudging Fast and Slow*, Cham, Switzerland: Palgrave Macmillan.

Tetlock, P.E., and Gardner, D. (2015), *Superforecasting: The Art and Science of Prediction*, New York: Crown.

Van Syckle, K. (2018), 'What It's Like to Report About the Porn Industry', *New York Times*, 26 March 2018.

Chapter 7: Safety in Numbers

Akerlof, G.A., and Shiller, R.J. (2016), *Phishing for Phools: The Economics of Manipulation and Deception*, Princeton, NJ: Princeton University Press.

Fama, E.F. (1965), *Random Walks in Stock-Market Prices*, Chicago: Graduate School of Business, University of Chicago.

Illing, S. (2018), 'Why We Pretend to Know Things, Explained by a Cognitive Scientist', *Vox*. Available from: https://www.vox.com/conversations/2017/3/2/14750464/truth-facts-psychology-donald-trump-knowledge-science

Isaac, R.M., Walker, J.M., Williams, A.W. (1994), 'Group Size and the Voluntary Provision of Public Goods: Experimental Evidence Utilizing Large Groups', *Journal of Public Economics*, 54(1): 1–36.

Marwell, G., and Ames, R.E. (1981), 'Economists Free Ride, Does Anyone Else?: Experiments on the Provision of Public Goods, IV', *Journal of Public Economics*, 15(3): 295–310.

Pressman, S. (2018), 'Hyman Minsky and Behavioral Finance', *Journal of Behavioral Economics for Policy*, 2(1): 33–37.

Shiller, R.J. (2003), 'From Efficient Markets Theory to Behavioral Finance'. Available from: https://www.nobelprize.org/uploads/2018/06/shiller-lecture.pdf

Van Wolkenten, M., Brosnan, S.F., de Waal, F.B. (2007), 'Inequity Responses of Monkeys Modified by Effort', *Proceedings of the National Academy of Sciences*, 104: 18854–9.

Chapter 8: The Big Picture

Akerlof, G.A. (1970), 'The Market for "Lemons": Quality Uncertainty and the Market Mechanism', *Quarterly Journal of Economics*, 84(3): 488–500.

Busemeyer, J., and Bruza, P. (2012), *Quantum Models of Cognition and Decision*, Cambridge: Cambridge University Press.

Cochrane, J. (2015), 'Homo economicus or Homo paleas?'. Available from: http://johnhcochrane.blogspot.ca/2015/05/homo-economicus-or-homo-paleas.html

Der Derian, J., and Wendt, A. (eds) (2021), *Quantizing International Relations*, Oxford: Oxford University Press (forthcoming).

O'Brien, H. (2019), 'Cass Sunstein and the Rise and Fall of Nudge Theory', *New Statesman*, 22 May 2019.

Orrell, D. (2018), *Quantum Economics: The New Science of Money*, London: Icon Books.

Orrell, D. (2020), *Quantum Economics and Finance: An Applied Mathematics Introduction*, Oxford: Panda Ohana.

Sunstein, C. (2014), 'Nudging: A Very Short Guide', *Journal of Consumer Policy*, 37(4): 583–588.

Timms, A. (2019), 'The Sameness of Cass Sunstein', *New Republic*, 20 June 2019.

Wendt, A. (2015), *Quantum Mind and Social Science: Unifying Physical and Social Ontology*, Cambridge: Cambridge University Press.

INDEX

ALSO AVAILABLE

In *Economyths*, David Orrell reveals the key myths on which mainstream economics is based – such as fair competition, rational behaviour, stability and eternal growth – and how these myths lead paradoxically to their opposites: inequality, an irrational economy, financial instability and a collision with nature's limits. He explores how economics is being reinvented through new ideas in mathematics, psychology and environmentalism – and, in this revised edition, the emerging field of quantum economics.

9781785782299 (paperback) / 9781785782442 (ebook)

Amid growing consensus that economics needs to go back to the drawing board, David Orrell argues that understanding the quantum nature of money is the key to revolutionising the discipline. From quantum physics to the dualistic properties of money, via the emerging areas of quantum finance and quantum cognition, this profoundly important book reveals that quantum economics is to neoclassical economics what quantum physics is to classical physics – a genuine turning point in our understanding.

9781785785085 (paperback) / 9781785784002 (ebook)